IMPROVING HUMAN PERFORMANCE SERIES

Jack Phillips, Ph.D., Series Editor

Accountability in Human Resource Management
Jack Phillips

The Adult Learner, 5th Edition
Malcolm Knowles and Elwood Holton

Handbook of Training Evaluation and Measurement Methods, 3rd Edition
Jack Phillips

The Power of 360° Feedback
David Waldman and Leanne Atwater

Return on Investment in Training and Performance Improvement Programs
Jack Phillips

Technology-Based Training
Serge Ravet and Maureen Layte

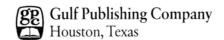
Gulf Publishing Company
Houston, Texas

THE POWER OF 360° FEEDBACK

How To
Leverage
Performance
Evaluations
For Top
Productivity

IMPROVING
HUMAN
PERFORMANCE
SERIES

DAVID A. WALDMAN, PH.D.
LEANNE E. ATWATER, PH.D.

The Power of 360° Feedback
How to Leverage Performance Evaluations for Top Productivity

Gulf Publishing Company
Book Division
P.O. Box 2608 □ Houston, Texas 77252-2608

10   9   8   7   6   5   4   3   2   1

Library of Congress Cataloging-in-Publication Data

Waldman, David A. (David Andrew), 1955–
    The power of 360° feedback : how to leverage performance
evaluations for top productivity / David A. Waldman and Leanne E.
Atwater.
        p.   cm.
    Includes bibliographical references and index.
    ISBN 0-88415-412-2 (alk. paper)
    1. Organizational effectiveness.   2. Corporate culture.   3. Feedback
(Psychology)   I. Atwater, Leanne E.   II. Title.
HD58.9.W35   1998
658.4'06–dc21   97-46343
                                                                    CIP

Transferred to Digital Printing 2007

*David Waldman dedicates this book
to his loving parents, Ida and Lester Waldman.
Their lifelong feedback and support have proved to be
invaluable, and he is forever grateful.*

*Leanne Atwater dedicates this book to her parents,
Clovis and Beryl Justice, for their encouragement,
generosity, and love, and to her husband, David,
who is "the wind beneath her wings."*

Contents

Acknowledgments

Acknowledgments are due to a number of individuals who have provided input and assistance. Our work in providing 360° feedback programs to various organizations could not have proceeded without the technical expertise of David Atwater. David has worked long and hard to provide user-friendly surveys and feedback reports. Our assistants, Priscilla Cartier and Kendra Pillsbury, help keep us organized and the data accurate— things that are obviously crucial for both good science and practice. A number of individuals have served as internal contacts and champions for the various organizations for which we have implemented 360° feedback. One such individual is Shelly Darcy, who also helped guide our earlier thinking regarding effective implementation processes. Finally, we tip our hats to the many individuals who have received formalized 360° feedback from us and especially those who have made honest attempts to change. Your involvement, enthusiasm, and courage have proved to be an inspiration.

Preface

Every ten years or so, a management innovation comes along that generates much enthusiasm in organizations. Three hundred sixty degree feedback has perhaps been the most notable management innovation of the 1990s. Literally thousands (and perhaps now more than a million) of individuals have received written feedback from sources once thought to be nontraditional or even taboo. These sources include subordinates, peers, and internal and external customers. The most obvious goal of 360° feedback is to increase one's self-awareness so one can improve in performance and in how one relates to the various sources mentioned above.

Numerous authors have written about 360° feedback in terms of what it is and how it should be implemented. Much less is known about how 360° feedback may, or may not, fit within an organizational context. Moreover, little is known about the effects of such feedback processes on organizations. How does 360° feedback alter an organization's culture? What is the impact, if any, on organizational performance? These and related questions have not been clearly addressed.

The purpose of this book is to address such questions and provide some answers, although caveats are occasionally put forth regarding the current lack of systematic knowledge of how 360° feedback may impact organizations. For example, research has only recently begun that attempts to link human resource strategies to organizational performance. We are aware of no research specifically attempting to link 360° feedback with performance, although this book makes a case for how such linkages should be expected to occur.

The book is based upon a scientist/practitioner model. This means it attempts to balance what is known from systematic scientific inquiry with what is known based on practice and experience. In addition, such an approach integrates scientifically generated knowledge with the needs of practitioners and managers working in field settings. Accordingly, we attempt to base prescriptions in this book on empirically based research or carefully formulated theory. The book also offers numerous practical examples for the purpose of joining together science and practice.

For whom did we write this book? We feel that it will be of interest to a variety of audiences. Senior managers and human resource decision makers will be interested because of the unique strategic perspective offered. The recent surge in 360° feedback programs has evolved with little systematic thinking regarding exactly why organizations have been rushing in this direction or even what they should expect to accomplish. Although the book raises some practical issues, it focuses on the strategic thinking that needs to coincide with implementation efforts. Without such thinking, implementation efforts will likely reap little in terms of benefits and may even result in harm to an organization. In short, the book makes the case that 360° feedback should be viewed as a long-term effort to enhance organizational change.

Academics constitute another targeted audience. The topic of 360° feedback is relevant to individuals teaching and doing research in industrial/organizational psychology and human resource management. We have attempted to provide material that not only yields practical insights but also is up-to-date with regard to research and theoretical thinking. The burgeoning literature about human resource strategies and organizational performance again serves as an example. We use recent theory and research from that literature to provide logical reasons as to how 360° feedback might impact performance. Unfortunately, actual research that focuses specifically on 360° feedback is lacking. We hope the ideas put forth in this book will stimulate more research. Perhaps even more importantly, we believe such research will be potentially more fruitful if conducted in terms of partnerships between academia and industry.

Furthermore, we hope this book reaches as many students as possible. It may be an excellent supplement for a human resource management course, as well as for courses in industrial/organizational psychology.

David A. Waldman, PhD.
Leanne E. Atwater, PhD.

CHAPTER 1

The Surge of 360°
Feedback Programs:
Benefits and Risks

"Followers don't know anything about leadership." These words came from a high-ranking U.S. Navy officer. He held the view that bosses know about leadership and are in the best position to judge whether a subordinate is a good leader. This wisdom prevailed in the late 1970s.

Managers and academics alike have come a long way in the past fifteen years in terms of their thinking about who should best evaluate leadership and, in fact, have begun to recognize that followers, peers, and customers, as well as superiors, know quite a bit about leadership. Even the U.S. Navy has made some progress in this area, although, like battleships, those old traditions do not die easily.

Today an estimated 20 to 25 percent of organizations actually ask followers, peers, and/or customers to rate managers, for developmental and learning purposes, and in some cases, performance evaluation purposes.[1] This approach to evaluation is referred to as 360° feedback. A similar though less inclusive process called upward feedback asks subordinates to rate superiors but does not include ratings from peers or customers.

Of *Fortune*'s thirty-two most-admired companies in 1994, twenty were using upward (followers rating leaders) or 360° feedback, and two companies were implementing such programs. Indeed, *Fortune* 500 companies spend hundreds of millions of dollars annually for feedback programs. In many ways, this has not only inverted the pyramid in that now managers look to employees for their input, but 360° feedback also asks for input from those above, that is, bosses; those below, or subordinates; those in comparable positions, that is, peers; and even internal and external customers. The term 360° refers to the circular view from all these positions around the target individual. Table 1-1 presents a list of companies that have adopted an upward or 360° feedback process for informing and/or evaluating managers. As can be seen, the types of organizations using 360° or upward feedback vary widely. Additionally, the process is not confined to the corporate giants; smaller companies as well are joining the trend.

At a basic level, the 360° feedback process usually involves the following steps. First, an organization identifies a number of managerial behaviors that it believes are important to its success and that others can observe. Next, each manager taking part in the process is rated by his or her followers, peers, customers, and superiors on some type of scale, usually via anonymous survey. However, in the case of ratings by superiors, responses can only be anonymous if the manager has more than one boss. Finally, the manager receives the survey responses in a report. Often, the average score for each group of raters appears on the report. As a result, raters get the opportunity to anonymously evaluate a manager, and the manager receives this feedback as information he or she might want to incorporate into future behaviors. Numerous variations exist regarding matters such as length and type of survey, how anonymity is assured, whether managers provide self-reports, how reports are prepared, how feedback is provided, subsequent management training, and follow-up. However, the primary goal is generally the same, that is, to improve leadership/management.

SAMPLE CASES

As noted above, the implementation of 360° feedback has grown steadily. It is beyond the scope of this book to cite all the existing cases, and indeed, not all have been researched or documented. However, some examples will be briefly described here to give the reader a quick feel for 360° feedback, including where it has been implemented and what it should accomplish.

Table 1-1
Companies That Have Recently Used 360° or Upward Feedback

Acuson Inc.	Levi Strauss
Alcoa	Libby-Owens-Ford Co.
Amoco	Limited Credit Services
AT&T	Lockheed Martin
Ball-InCon	Massachusetts Mutual Life
Bank of America	Insurance Co.
Bell South	Merck
Ben & Jerry's	Motorola
Borden Foods	Nestlé
Caterpillar	Nortel Inc.
Chase Manhattan Bank	Pacific Gas and Electric
Chrysler	Pitney Bowes
Colgate-Palmolive Co.	PRC (of Litton Industries)
Deloitte & Touche	Proctor and Gamble
Consulting Group	Raychem Corp.
Disney	Rhone-Poulenc Agriculture
DuPont	Scottsdale Insurance
Eastman Kodak Co.	Shell Oil
Exxon	Stride Rite Corp.
FAA	Syntex
Federal Express Corp.	Tenneco
Ford Motor Company	Texaco
General Mills	3M
General Motors	TRW
GTE Corp.	United Airlines
Heller Financial	UPS
Hewlett Packard	Warner-Lambert Co.
IBM	Wells Fargo Bank
Johnson & Johnson	World Bank
Kaiser Permanente	Xerox

Heller Financial in Chicago attempted to implement 360° feedback in the late 1980s as a means of building a more empowered culture.[2] Heller's executive team feared the culture that existed at the time was unparticipative and did not encourage speedy responses to customer needs. At the same time, the company wanted to maintain a strong results orientation. An upward feedback process was launched at top management levels and eventually cascaded to lower levels, with the goal of increasing participation by giving subordinates the chance to provide feedback to their managers.

Other similar examples abound. Ball-InCon, a glass manufacturer in Indiana, adopted a combination of subordinate and peer feedback in an attempt to build quality and empowerment deep into the company's culture.[3] Similarly, Motorola has used 360° feedback to ensure that executive behavior aligns with the company's values and culture. AT&T has put thousands of managers through an upward and/or broader 360° feedback process in recent years. For example, at AT&T's business products division, any manager supervising three or more employees goes through an annual 360° feedback process and must share the results with colleagues both up and down the organizational hierarchy.[4] The Arizona Department of Public Safety, which includes the state's highway patrol, has implemented upward feedback with its police leaders in an attempt to increase empowerment and promote a prevention-oriented, problem-solving approach to policing. As the examples above illustrate, 360° feedback can help accomplish a variety of goals, including leadership development, culture change, and increased participation. Companies can also encourage specific desired behaviors by designing survey items to address target areas.

In sum, 360° feedback has spread quickly across the organizational landscape. However, questions remain as to exactly what such feedback efforts can be reasonably expected to accomplish and under what conditions. To understand why 360° feedback has become so popular, as well as its potential for success—and, as will be seen, potential for failure—360° feedback must be placed within a strategic and organizational context.

360° FEEDBACK IN CONTEXT

A key theme of this book is the need for each organization that is considering the implementation of 360° feedback to understand its 360° feedback program within a context. Two issues are relevant to context. First, 360° feedback is in line with recent management trends such as total quality management (TQM) and high-involvement organizations. Proponents of TQM have criticized traditional performance appraisal approaches, which place predominant emphasis on top-down feedback and evaluation. Broadening feedback input to include 360° sources would be more congruent with TQM. Moreover, proponents of high-involvement organizations have extolled the virtues of gaining more input from employees. Organizations need mechanisms or programs to make high involvement come to life. A formalized 360° feedback program is one such mechanism.

Second, formalized 360° feedback can be considered an offshoot or close cousin of a more established type of organizational development (OD) program—survey/feedback. Indeed, survey/feedback has been around for a long time in organizations as a widescale technique associated with OD. Typically, the survey includes a wide range of attitudinal issues, including job satisfaction, work conditions, and benefits, as well as aspects of supervision or leadership. Management then uses this survey information to diagnose problems and design solutions.

Formalized 360° feedback is a type of survey feedback. It focuses specifically on the appraisal of managers by their subordinates, peers, customers, and superiors based on critical competencies associated with supervision or leadership. In addition, as compared with more established forms of survey/feedback, 360° feedback programs have more specific relevance to managers' performances and perhaps their evaluations and outcomes. Thus, with 360° feedback the target for change is clearly the manager, rather than organizational policies or job design issues.

FEEDBACK AND SELF-PERCEPTION

The rationale behind using 360° feedback to improve leadership/management rests with notions of self-perception. Feedback has been found to increase the accuracy of self-perception, as well as to give individuals information about how others perceive their behavior. This awareness can inform the leader about the need for behavior change. If the leader never receives feedback, the self-perception may remain inaccurate or uninformed, and thus the leader does not make necessary behavior modifications.

For example, Raychem's CEO Robert Saldich obtained feedback from his team revealing that his subordinates were aware of his weakness in contingency planning, something he thought he had kept well hidden. Joe Malik, manager of a team of engineers at AT&T, got nicked for his vigorous temper, which was not a big revelation to him. However, Malik was surprised to learn through upward feedback that his subordinates expected him to articulate the vision of the unit, something he had never imagined his people wanted.[5]

A long history of research suggests that people do not evaluate themselves accurately—or at least not in line with how others view them. Numerous researchers have documented that self-ratings of behavior, personality, and other job performance categories suffer from unreliability and bias, and generally are suspect and inaccurate when compared with ratings provided by others or with other objective measures.[6] And generally—although not always—the self-perceptions people have reflect positive biases.

Self-perception is often inaccurate because of a lack of information, fueled by individuals' tendencies to withhold negative feedback from others. It is well documented that most individuals do not enjoy giving or find it inappropriate to give others negative feedback. Thus, they avoid it. As a consequence, most people receive less negative feedback than is realistic, and what they do receive often has a sugar coating. This contributes to a tendency for individuals to see themselves in an unrealistically positive light. For example, William McKiernan of Colgate-Palmolive indicated that many of the firm's managers thought they knew how colleagues and subordinates viewed them, but when the managers received their feedback, they were shocked. They reported feeling quite disconcerted to learn that others saw them as inflexible or as individuals who refused to share information.

Inaccurate self-perception also can result because individuals tend to discount or rationalize negative feedback. Positive feedback is generally more accepted as accurate and informational than negative feedback.[7] This is particularly true of individuals with high self-esteem or narcissistic personalities. This tendency also may occur because positive information aligns more consistently with individuals' self-perceptions. However, some researchers have found that managers report stronger intentions to change and put forth more effort toward change when they have received negative feedback. When the negative information comes in the form of anonymous feedback from a number of individuals about specific behaviors, it is more difficult to discount or deny and therefore may more likely be accepted.

Recent studies indicate that feedback can cause individuals to modify their self-evaluations.[8] Of course, others' evaluations are not always accurate, although others' ratings of performance tend to relate more closely to objective criteria than a person's own ratings do. Rather, the knowledge of how others perceive a person, particularly in terms of observable behavior and the impact of one's behavior on others, is valuable information to possess for a number of reasons. First, in some cases, observers' ratings may be more valid than self-ratings. For example, a person may believe she is friendly and approachable, while her peers find her unfriendly and difficult to approach. In this case, observers' judgments are more accurate, because what matters is their perception of her friendliness. Second, whether others' evaluations are accurate or inaccurate, in most work settings it is important to understand and acknowledge others' perceptions of oneself. For instance, subordinates' perceptions of their leader's behavior can influence their attitudes and behavior. Leaders who are unaware of how these observers perceive them have a disadvantage. Third, negative organizational consequences may result if individuals do not perceive themselves as others do. For example, when making decisions about the amount of effort required for a project or the allocation of one's time, self-assessments of strengths and weaknesses play an important role. If they are misjudged, individuals' abilities to successfully regulate their behavior are hampered.[9] Moreover, recent studies have suggested that individuals who provide inflated self-ratings relative to others' ratings are poorer performers and less effective than individuals who provide self-ratings in greater agreement with others' ratings.[10]

While 360° feedback is generally seen as valuable because of its informational benefits, such as suggesting weaknesses and misperceptions, 360° feedback can also have other benefits. Many of these benefits extend to the greater organization and thus will be the primary focus of this book. Because the organizational benefits of 360° feedback, as well as its potential hazards, have not been carefully considered, many organizations have rushed into such programs without fully understanding the possible or realistic impact 360° feedback programs may have on the organization as a whole. Moreover, executives and practitioners alike have not carefully considered the contextual factors that may determine the ultimate success of a 360° implementation effort. This book strives to provide a broader picture of the organizational context to help ensure effective implementation and realization of benefits. The potential benefits of 360° feedback include:

1. Enhanced organizational involvement of those asked to provide the feedback;

2. Positive reinforcement for leaders' good performances;

3. Greater interest in feedback on the part of leaders;

4. Better communication between leaders and their followers, peers, customers, and superiors;

5. Improvements in leader behaviors;

6. Change in organizational culture toward more participation and openness; and

7. Additional sources of input into the formal performance appraisal process.

These benefits, as well as potential hazards that can result if the 360° feedback process is not handled properly, are discussed in detail below.

BENEFITS OF USING 360° FEEDBACK

Employee Involvement

Most people at one time or another have wished for the opportunity to anonymously tell their bosses or co-workers how their behavior could improve. And often, had this opportunity surfaced, those bosses or co-workers could have been enlightened. In addition, when employees are asked to provide assessments it signals that the company believes employees have something valuable to contribute toward management improvement. But although much of the popular management literature in the last ten years has emphasized participation, empowerment, and customer satisfaction surveys, the message has not convinced many employees or customers that their input has true value. Three hundred sixty–degree feedback programs encourage employees and customers to believe they can impact their futures and the future of the organization by signaling that the organization values their input. Participation rates and anecdotal evidence suggest that when individuals are asked to participate in a 360° feedback process and *they trust that the feedback will be anonymous,* they are anxious to participate.

Federal Express uses an automated employee survey system called the Survey Feedback Action program, or SFA, to keep in touch with the workforce. The survey also includes a section for employees to evaluate their managers. Fed Ex believes SFA demonstrates the company's philosophy of putting employees first.

Positive Reinforcement of the Leader

Not all leaders receive negative feedback, or ratings lower than they expected. In fact, some receive more positive feedback than they antici- pated. In these cases, leaders receive positive reinforcement for the behav- iors their followers, peers, customers, or superiors desire from them. The second author of this book remembers waiting to receive student evaluations after her first semester of teaching. Incidentally, college faculty are among the few who have received upward feedback on a regular basis for years. As one of the few civilian female professors at the U.S. Naval Academy, she had just finished teaching an elective psychology course, and most of her students were male engineering majors. While she expected negative evaluations, they turned out very positive and personally reward- ing. She believes the emotional rewards received from feeling she had successfully taught that class likely influenced her decision to pursue an academic career.

The same can occur for managers who are unsure about their per- formance or their impact on followers or co-workers. Positive feedback can be very reinforcing, particularly if unexpected. This positive feedback can also be motivational in that the manager will not want to let followers down; the manager will want to live up to their expectations in the future.

Surprisingly, many managers with whom the authors have spoken in recent years reported that they never received formal feedback from anyone other than a boss, and even that feedback was often rare or uninformative. Traditional performance appraisal has relied on superiors to identify rele- vant behaviors and provide specific feedback, but this rarely occurs. Conse- quently, many managers have spent twenty years or more managing without ever getting specific feedback about their strengths and weaknesses.

Increased Interest in Feedback

One of the side benefits of providing feedback is leaders' increased interest in subsequent feedback. Often, after receiving feedback, leaders are motivated to make changes and, after attempting those changes, are interested in subsequent feedback to see if others have perceived and appreciated the changes. This interest in feedback can have many long- term benefits even if formal 360° feedback is discontinued, because it has sensitized the leader to the value of feedback. The leader will therefore more likely seek it in the future.

Improved Communication Between Leaders and Others

Many steps in the 360° feedback process can facilitate communication between leaders and their followers, peers, customers, and superiors. Specifically, as this book will later advocate, 360° feedback reports should be followed by solicitations of additional clarification from rater groups. Todd White, former CEO of the management consulting firm Blessing/White Inc., states that "the real value of reverse reviews for a manager is not just getting the feedback, but in discussing it with subordinates."[11]

For example, the leader can meet with the followers as a group or individually to acquire additional, more specific information about the feedback he or she received. In these meetings, the leader also can provide information to followers about the group's responses. These clarification meetings can be quite beneficial for improving communication because the meetings solicit two-way communication. That is, rather than the leader providing information in a vertical, downward fashion, communication goes both up and down. In addition, it is uncommon for managers to hold meetings to discuss their own styles or behaviors. Thus, a whole new area is often explored. Also, the personal nature of the communication in these meetings—that is, discussing the manager's strengths and weaknesses—can break down communication barriers. Chapter 6 describes the experiences the authors had facilitating these processes with a top executive.

Steps Toward Organizational Culture Change

As mentioned earlier, many companies have introduced upward or 360° feedback as a step toward a more participative and empowering organizational culture. Asking employees and customers to provide feedback to their managers signals that the organization believes the employees and customers have information of value to contribute. It also suggests to managers that the organization takes interest in how they manage people. In other words, it is not only getting results, but *how* managers get those results that matters. Implementing 360° feedback—and suggesting to managers that they should be accountable to their constituents—can be a very new concept in some organizations in which traditional, hierarchical management has been the norm. A major restructuring in the early 1990s and a move to a TQM-based culture prompted a division of Litton Industries to incorporate 360° feedback as part of its new value-based human resource system. Litton's philosophy—producing results is not enough unless it is done in the right man-ner—was promoted by 360° feedback. In other words, results at the expense of employee morale or satisfaction was not acceptable. Ultimately, Litton included 360° ratings as part of its managerial appraisal process.

The forum for conversation and discussion of expectations created by the 360° feedback process also creates opportunities for sharing and clari-fying the organization's values. Often individuals question why they have particular expectations and why they behave in particular ways. This process of questioning illuminates individuals' beliefs and values, which may or may not align with those of the organization's culture. Increasingly, chief executives use 360° feedback processes to spread their own visions of their companies and reinforce new corporate values. When CEO Melvin Goodes of Warner-Lambert articulated the company's values, a 360° feedback process was designed around the vision and values, thus embracing the old notion that companies get what they measure.

Additional Sources of Input Into the Performance Appraisal Process

Controversy abounds about incorporating 360° feedback ratings into managers' performance evaluations. Three primary approaches to this issue exist. Some believe that using ratings for evaluative as opposed to strictly developmental purposes ruins the feedback process. They cite a number of problems. These include dishonest rating (when raters believe they can influence managers' outcomes), game playing, and managers per-forming to the ratings.

Others maintain that companies can incorporate 360° feedback into appraisal after a period of adjustment. Incorporating the 360° feedback process into an organization is a major organizational change. These pro-ponents believe that both raters and managers should accustom them-selves to the process before the company uses it for evaluation, but that over time—perhaps two to three years—360° ratings can provide valuable information in the evaluation process and should serve as part of man-agers' performance evaluations.

A third group believes that if 360° feedback is to be taken seriously and if companies expect managers to respond by changing their behav-iors, managers must be held accountable by making 360° ratings part of the appraisal process. Federal Express and Litton are just two examples of companies that have incorporated 360° or upward ratings into appraisal processes. If this approach is taken, the company must address a number of issues regarding exactly how to incorporate the information. For example, are employee or customer ratings weighted equally with superior ratings? Are employee ratings used as the sole measures for some aspects of performance? Are employee or peer ratings given to the manager's superior for use at his or her discretion in the evaluation? What are the legal ramifications of using anonymous, unverifiable feedback for reward or discipline decisions? Chapter 3 discusses these issues in greater detail.

In sum, most who have implemented the 360° process believe it has numerous potential benefits. This does not mean, however, that it poses no potential hazards or risks, as discussed in the next section.

POTENTIAL HAZARDS OF USING 360° FEEDBACK

Retribution

A primary concern voiced by employees about 360° feedback is the fear of retaliation or retribution by managers who receive poor ratings. Many employees express concern that their feedback will not really be anonymous. For example, if the ratings are consistently low, the manager will know each of his or her employees or peers gave low ratings. Will the manager then punish employees in some way in retaliation or in hopes of threatening employees into providing higher ratings in the future? In the case of peer feedback, will relationships among peers deteriorate or become vengeful?

Most companies go to great lengths to ensure anonymity. For example, some do not provide feedback reports to managers unless the manager has a sufficient number of raters—perhaps three, four, or five. Others use outside consultants for data collection and dissemination so no one within the company has access to individual data. Nevertheless, fears of retaliation are occasionally realized. And even the fears themselves, whether founded or not, can pose problems if they cause individuals to provide dishonest ratings.

Defensiveness and Denial

Perhaps a less dangerous hazard concerns the denial of the ratings by the manager. In one vivid case, a manager accused the consultants providing the feedback of giving him a false report and questioned their motives for doing so. He was completely convinced that the ratings and write-in comments he had received were not his and that the consultants had manufactured them for some sinister purpose. Interestingly, the comments he denied included some suggesting he was paranoid at times.

Even in less extreme cases, denial and defensiveness can present problems. For one thing, unless the manager acknowledges the feedback as valid, he or she will make little attempt to make any changes. Additionally, defensiveness may create barriers to acknowledging future feedback received via 360° feedback results or more informally from other encounters.

Generally, denial and defensiveness can be minimized if the feedback is presented properly. Most experts agree that the feedback should be accompanied by counseling, training, or attempts to facilitate the interpretation of the feedback. Trained facilitators should perform this counseling, preferably in person. One benefit of doing feedback sessions in groups is that managers will less often deny the validity of the feedback or become defensive when they realize they are not the only ones with low scores. In other words, merely sending a manager his or her feedback report with no discussion would more likely result in denial or defensiveness than feedback provided in a supportive training session.

Conflicting Ratings

What should a manager do if he or she receives high, or positive, scores on a particular dimension from a superior but low, or negative, scores on that dimension from subordinates? Without the aid of a facilitator, the manager could easily discount the data as invalid. The facilitator can help the manager identify the different behaviors the two groups have observed or understand the different expectations and perspectives of the two groups. The manager needs to see both ratings as valid, understand the discrepancy, and formulate action plans targeted specifically toward improved relationships with both groups.

Lowered Self-esteem

Receiving feedback that is much more negative than expected can be quite a blow to a manager's self-esteem. Given that most people have inflated self-perceptions and have received less negative feedback than perhaps they should have, receiving feedback from subordinates that is more negative than anticipated often comes unexpectedly and unpleasantly. In feedback sessions, some managers have actually left the room in tears or have come close to tears after receiving unexpected negative feedback. One woman tearfully explained that getting negative feedback from her subordinates was like being told she was a bad mother by her children. A lowering of a manager's self-esteem, such as thoughts of reduced capabilities or competence, may result. In most cases these negative self-feelings are temporary. In fact, they generally begin to subside in a day or two, and the manager responds with an action plan to improve. However, in an isolated case now and then the feedback may be so devastating that the individual's self-esteem does not quickly recover. In this case, further intervention with this individual may be necessary.

Game Playing

As presented briefly above in the discussion of performance appraisal, 360° feedback ratings occasionally promote game playing on the part of employees, peers, or managers. The authors recently conducted a feedback session in which a manager who had received high ratings jokingly remarked, "I guess those hundred-dollar bills weren't wasted after all." Although said with tongue in cheek, one can envision perhaps less overt game-playing activities. Some concern exists, particularly if ratings are used to influence managers' outcomes or if others will see the ratings, that managers will try to subtly increase ratings. They may do this by temporarily altering their behavior just before the rating period, by "kissing up" to employees, or even by subtly threatening employees. Comments such as "I sure hope I don't see any poor scores on this feedback survey" can artificially inflate a manager's scores.

Employees are also not exempt from game playing. The authors have heard employees say they would give their managers, who the employees believe have treated them badly, low ratings just to get even. Additionally, some co-workers indicate they would do just the opposite by providing artificially high ratings because their managers are also their friends; the co-workers don't want to hurt their friends' feelings or negatively impact their jobs or careers, even if they aren't the greatest managers.

Two primary hazards result from dishonest feedback. First, inflated, or insincerely positive, feedback allows managers to believe they have strengths they do not possess. This feedback may reconfirm inaccurate positive self-perceptions, which then become even more difficult to alter in the future. Deflated, or insincerely negative, feedback inaccurately criticizes managers for weaknesses that do not really exist. Therefore, future efforts may be wasted in areas that need no additional improvement. If the feedback system is implemented optimally, incidents of dishonest feedback can be greatly reduced.

When 360° feedback is truly anonymous and used for developmental purposes, not evaluative decisions, these games become much less common. Most employees see the 360° feedback process as an opportunity to provide information that may improve their managers' performances—and perhaps their own job satisfaction—or the performances of their organizations.

Time and Money

The introduction of 360° feedback is not free. Costs include designing 360° feedback instruments, collecting data, preparing feedback reports, and training the managers receiving feedback. Costs also exist in terms of employee time to complete surveys and to attend meetings and training sessions. One of the most recent criticisms of 360° feedback concerns the lack of studies assessing its impact on the bottom line. In fact, like the multitude of other human resource initiatives in the past, it may be difficult to determine the true cost-benefits of 360° feedback or specific managerial improvements made as a result of the feedback. Reductions in turnover or lower grievance rates might be the easiest to document, but concluding that 360° feedback caused these reductions is difficult to demonstrate because no intervention exists in a vacuum. Other things always occur, both within and outside the organization, that can impact outcomes.

As such, most studies claiming positive impacts have relied on perceptual measures rather than hard numbers. The fact that 360° feedback effects may take quite some time to realize also inhibits a quick cost-benefit assessment. Like many organizational change efforts, cultures and habits do not change quickly. Those who embark on 360° feedback programs should realize that the costs to implement the process may be easier to show on paper than the benefits that result, particularly in the short term.

Increased Expectations Coupled With Lack of Change

Once an individual expresses a suggestion for improvement, that person tends to believe the suggestion provided should actually result in change. It is often not that simple. In some cases, organizational goals, policies, or procedures may prohibit change. Or perhaps that individual held an uncommon opinion about what changes were necessary. And it is always possible the manager will not respond to the suggestions. Regardless, lessons learned from employee opinion surveys show that when employees express their dissatisfactions, they expect remedies. Similarly, elevated expectations result from 360° feedback programs. If no improvements result, employee dissatisfaction may increase when heightened expectations for change are not realized.

Unfortunately, a possibility that behavior changes will not result does exist among managers who receive 360° feedback. As mentioned earlier, behavior patterns, reward systems, and cultures do not change easily. Unless many changes occur simultaneously to support behavior change, such as training for managers, and a sense of true commitment to the changes exists, improvements may be short-lived or never seen.

Faddism

One skeptical manager recently indicated that he feared 360° feedback was the flavor of the month. He and others had seen many programs come and go, and they feared 360° feedback was just another program that would be here today and gone tomorrow. They also feared the 360° feedback process would raise employees' expectations and then management would just let it die.

This is not an uncommon fear. Everyone has seen initiatives such as MBO, quality circles, job enrichment, and total quality come and go. Some remain skeptical that 360° feedback will not have a similar fate. This type of cynicism, even when unfounded, can undermine any program, including the 360° feedback process. The why-should-I-bother mentality influences the degree to which employees participate, as well as the commitment of managers to the possibilities of improvement. John Kotter in a recent issue of *Harvard Business Review* indicated that one of the problems organizations face in successfully implementing change is they do not express a strong enough sense of urgency for change, nor do they thoroughly breathe the change into everything they do over time.[12]

Much of this book will address the issue of viewing 360° feedback in the context of a strategic organizational transformation. If this does not occur, 360° feedback could indeed take on the appearance of a fad and thus lose much of its potential value. Chapter 2 discusses the faddism issue in more detail.

What Follows Feedback?

Feedback provides information to managers. But information alone does not change behavior. In fact, many other factors affect the extent to which managers incorporate the information into behavior. These factors include the duration of contemplation—it takes time to digest feedback and form realistic action plans—goal setting, organizational overdetermination, resistance to change, organizational reward systems, and others. This book will discuss each of these factors in detail later.

PLAN OF THE BOOK

As the reader has probably gleaned from this introduction, successfully implementing 360° feedback is not a simple process, and positive outcomes are not guaranteed. Many issues must be addressed if the intervention is to go well. These issues pertain largely to an organization's strategic context. This book goes into detail about how to optimize the benefits and minimize the risks by focusing attention on the context in which 360° feedback occurs.

Chapter 2 begins by discussing how 360° feedback should be considered a significant organizational change effort. It challenges the values of existing hierarchical organizations in many ways. It also requires a systematic top-down approach that considers both technical and social systems in the organization.

Chapter 3 outlines the specifics of a strategic context and how it relates to effective 360° feedback implementation. For illustration purposes, the authors will present the results of an in-depth case study and interview research conducted regarding 360° feedback practices in organizations. Regarding the interviews, the authors contacted a number of practitioners and asked them about current practices—especially about implementation problems. The results should prove enlightening in providing insight into the nature of common problems and potential solutions. Also, Chapter 3 provides arguments for piloting any proposed, large-scale implementation before it is rolled out. Recent experiences of the authors in a large division of a multinational telecommunication firm provide an illustrative case study.

Chapter 4 carefully considers why organizations implement 360° feedback. It considers the genuine desire companies have to increase managerial effectiveness via 360° feedback. But at the same time, the authors draw on institutional theory to discuss potential copycat motives. A model highlights the process whereby 360° feedback can be expected to impact organizations, with changes in organizational culture preceding performance improvement.

Individual performance as impacted by feedback provides the subject for Chapter 5. This chapter focuses on the importance of accurate self-perception in work settings, as well as the factors that influence acceptance of feedback and the motivation to change. Also discussed are the outcomes one can expect when ratings by self and ratings by others differ greatly, for example, the performance implications when a manager receives feedback more positive than expected versus more negative.

Chapter 6 delves into the connection between 360° feedback and organizational culture. This connection provides the key to understanding how to ultimately link 360° feedback to performance, an issue also addressed in Chapter 7. Organizational culture impacts and is impacted by 360° feedback, and Chapter 6 elucidates this push-pull phenomenon. At the same time, the chapter raises cautions about the possible downsides of such feedback programs and how they may affect organizational culture. For example, will managers maintain high performance standards for employees if they know upward feedback provided by employees could be included as part of the managers' formal performance appraisal? Will the "the-customer-is-always-right" adage hold in reference to 360° ratings? Will employee fear and disillusionment grow if an attempt is made to link customer feedback with employee appraisals? Chapter 6 presents examples and anecdotes to address these questions. It also suggests ways to avoid doing potential damage to the organizational culture.

Ultimately, managers and stakeholders in the organization will want to see improvement that has resulted from the 360° feedback process. In other words, individuals will ask, "How well is this working?" The extent to which 360° feedback impacts organizational performance provides the main topic for Chapter 7. The chapter summarizes available research and the potential process by which organizational performance changes can be expected to take place, as well as offering specific recommendations for additional research.

The book concludes with a consideration of the future of 360° feedback in Chapter 8. No one has a crystal ball. However, certain trends indicate the process's possible future. Three hundred sixty–degree feedback will not remain effective unless it is continuously improved and allowed to evolve. As an example, as an organization matures in its two-way communication processes, a time may come when it has little need for *formal* 360° feedback, which is the type described in this book. In such a case, the organization might reserve formal 360° feedback for new managers. For more-experienced managers, open-door policies might efficiently promote effective feedback. However, this scenario requires an open and trusting environment, generally not the norm in businesses today. A concluding discussion clarifies how organizations can yield the benefits of 360° feedback as an emerging science, rather than a dying fad.

In summary, this book covers key topics relevant to assessing whether 360° feedback will serve an organization's needs, and if so, how it can be implemented and maintained to optimize managerial and organizational performance.

REFERENCES

1. For more information regarding the general usage of 360° feedback, see D. Antonioni, "Designing an Effective 360° Appraisal Feedback Process," *Organizational Dynamics* (in press).
2. For more information on this case, see K. Ludeman, "Upward Feedback Helps Managers Walk the Talk," *HR Magazine* (May 1993), pp. 85–88, 92–93.
3. Ibid.
4. Example taken from B. O'Reilly, "360-Degree Feedback Can Change Your Life," *Fortune* (October 17, 1994), pp. 93–94, 96, 100.
5. Ibid.
6. See:
   M. Harris and J. Schaubroeck, "A Meta-analysis of Self-Supervisor, Self-Peer, and Peer-Supervisor Ratings," *Personnel Psychology*, 41 (1988), pp. 43–61.
   P. Mabe and S. West, "Validity of Self-evaluation of Ability: A Review and Meta-analysis," *Journal of Applied Psychology*, 67 (1982), pp. 280–296.

7. See D. Ilgen, C. Fisher, and M. Taylor, "Consequences of Individual Feedback on Behavior in Organizations," *Journal of Applied Psychology,* 64 (1979), pp. 4, 349–371.
8. See L. Atwater, P. Roush, and A. Fischthal, "The Influence of Upward Feedback on Self- and Follower Ratings of Leadership," *Personnel Psychology,* 48 (1995), pp. 35–59.
9. See M. Taylor, C. Fisher, and D. Ilgen, "Individuals' Reactions to Performance Feedback in Organizations: A Control Theory Perspective," *Research in Personnel and Human Resources Management,* 2 (1986), pp. 81–124.
10. See for example:

L. Atwater and F. Yammarino, "Does Self-Other Agreement on Leadership Perceptions Moderate the Validity of Leadership and Performance Predictions?" *Personnel Psychology,* 45 (1992), pp. 141–164.

B. Bass and F. Yammarino, "Congruence of Self- and Others' Leadership Ratings of Naval Officers for Understanding Successful Performance," *Applied Psychology: An International Review,* 40 (1991), pp. 437–454.

E. Van Velsor, S. Taylor, and J. Leslie, "Self-Rater Agreement, Self-awareness, and Leadership Effectiveness," (paper presented at the annual convention of the American Psychological Association in Washington, D.C., August 1992).

F. Yammarino and L. Atwater, "Understanding Self-perception Accuracy: Implications for Human Resources Management," *Human Resource Management,* 32 (1993), pp. 231–247.

Atwater, Roush, and Fischthal, op cit.
11. M. Budman and B. Rice, "The Rating Game," *Across the Board,* 31(2) (February 1994), p. 37.
12. John Kotter, "Leading Change: Why Transformation Efforts Fail," *Harvard Business Review* (March–April 1995), pp. 59–67.

CHAPTER 2

HR Innovation vs. Organizational Change Effort

Will the fast-growing popularity of 360° feedback in the organizational world ultimately lead to its being relegated to the less-than-distinguished label of *fad*? Will it join a long line of other fads that psychologists and human resource specialists have made popular during the past 30 years? In the 1960s, the craze was t-groups and sensitivity training. Managers learned to share their feelings and perceptions of others in an artificial group setting. The 1970s brought in such fads as quality circles and attitude surveys. The 1980s were consumed by job enrichment and autonomous work groups. The latter continues to be popular perhaps because of the inherent changes in organizations that team-based structures entail. However, in general, most of these initiatives have experienced various degrees of success and a gradual fizzling of their faddish statuses.

The purpose here is to identify reasons why initiatives such as formalized 360° feedback can turn into fads. Furthermore, this chapter presents an implementation perspective that could help organizations avoid such fates. In sum, the authors hope that through effective strategizing and planning, 360° feedback will continue to be seen as a useful tool in organizations, rather than another short-term management fad.

The current enthusiasm over 360° feedback seems to occur for two key reasons. First, as mentioned earlier, 360° feedback has a content and procedure similar to more established forms of survey/feedback and, as such, does not represent a totally new or startling process.

Second, 360° feedback is very much in line with the notion of high-involvement organizations.[1] In other words, it provides a formal mechanism for employees and customers to help shape the leadership direction of the firm. More and more data have shown employee involvement in decision making and feedback processes to be an important element of organizational success.[2] For example, if managers do not provide appropriate leadership, feedback from subordinates can presumably make this known so remedial actions such as leadership development can be taken.

Upward feedback also aligns with the inverted pyramid, which places external customers at the top, followed by employees, and then management. By using the inverted pyramid concept, managers and employees work more in collaboration compared with traditional organizations, in which managers form the top of the pyramid, followed by employees, and then customers.[3] According to the inverted pyramid, managers should support or facilitate the efforts of employees. Employees should, in turn, serve customers. It then makes sense that at least some of the feedback managers receive should come directly from employees. This feedback should provide information as to whether managerial behavior truly supports employees.

For the most part, previous initiatives that became referred to as fads have experienced cycles. That is, they reached their peaks and then entered a steady but declining trend of implementation. Has formalized 360° feedback reached its peak? Will it gradually go by the wayside like so many management fads of the past? Is this peak-and-decline phenomenon natural, and what forces may be pushing 360° feedback in the decline direction? The material below addresses these questions and gives insights as to how 360° feedback, if treated as a facilitator to an organizational change effort, might avoid the fad syndrome and maintain long-term application in organizations.

New Appraisal Technique or Organizational Change Effort?

Some people might be tempted to classify recent uses of 360° feedback as simply new approaches to performance appraisal. During the past few decades, many new applications have appeared in the appraisal arena, including management-by-objectives (MBO), self-appraisal, behaviorally anchored rating scales (BARS), and behavior observation scales (BOS). Perhaps 360° feedback should simply be thrown into this group. For a moment, the authors will play devil's advocate and consider implementation issues from a tactical viewpoint that XYZ Company might consider in its attempt to implement a 360° feedback program.

First, XYZ should take proper psychometric steps to determine the dimensions to measure on the 360° survey, either generically across organizations or specifically within a given organization. As well, the company would have to determine appropriate scaling procedures. Questions such as the following would take center stage as the XYZ Company made implementation decisions:

1. Should a typical, five-point Likert scale (ranging from strongly agree to strongly disagree) be used?

2. Should a neutral point be provided, or should raters be forced to make either positive or negative evaluations?

3. Are appropriate off-the-shelf measures available?

Second, there is the problem of how to administer a 360° appraisal process and then provide feedback. XYZ would likely turn to consultants, and indeed, many consulting groups offer packages to assist companies in implementing upward or 360° feedback programs. Typically, the consultant would send an established survey—one that has been devised, validated, and normed across many organizational settings—to a group of individuals from XYZ Company. These individuals would then rate their respective managers. Completed surveys would then come back to the external consultant, who would process them off-site and produce an elaborate feedback report for each targeted manager. Alternatively, to speed up the process, respondents could input 360° ratings directly by computer/phone linkages.

Sometimes this process accompanies a leadership development program also marketed by the consultant. Thus, feedback may be given at a one-shot seminar to a group of managers who have been surveyed. This approach allows many managers to be "developed" simultaneously, which is of interest as more and more firms attempt to implement 360° feedback on a more widespread and continual basis.

The above implementation methods may seem logical and appear to form the basis of a tidy program for an organization wishing to pursue 360° appraisal. Indeed, important reasons exist as to why decisions would ultimately have to be made concerning the tactical issues raised above. At the same time, however, the authors view this typical sequence of events as a recipe for faddism and potential disappointment for client organizations.

The reasoning for this conclusion is described below and elaborated in subsequent chapters. The next chapter presents the results of interviews conducted by the authors that explore problems organizations face as they implement 360° feedback programs. In addition, the authors will describe their own experiences, including a case study that illustrates an approach that may increase the chances of effective long-term implementation.

WHAT'S WRONG WITH THIS PICTURE?

Three hundred sixty–degree feedback is not an innocuous process. For managers, it represents a dramatic shift in the organizational power structure, especially if ratings are used in any evaluative manner. A traditional pyramid-shaped organization places the responsibility and privilege of evaluation in the hands of managers, not subordinates, peers, or even customers. Any change in this seemingly natural order will not be taken lightly, even by the most enlightened of managers. Additionally, managers do not always welcome feedback from subordinates, fearing negative input or retribution.

Managers' distrust is heightened by the predominant policy of anonymity for 360° input sources. While anonymity may be necessary to ensure cooperation by feedback providers, it nevertheless may engender distrust on the part of feedback recipients for two reasons. First, the information is not verifiable. In a traditional appraisal system, the data come only from one's supervisor, and indeed, appraisal forms typically bear the supervisor's signature. Such is not the case with 360° appraisals; they are typically aggregated to form a composite score(s). Second, anonymity tends to obscure feedback. When a manager knows who is providing feedback, the rater may provide examples and particular concerns, which can help clarify what the manager needs to do to improve. Managers want to know who said what so they can deal with the issues on a one-to-one basis. In the case of 360° feedback, the manager only receives scores from anonymous raters and may not know why those scores occurred. In short, lack of verifiability and specificity add to many managers' skepticism of 360° feedback. Unfortunately, such skepticism reduces the possibility of effective implementation.[4]

Yes, it is true that organizations have become increasingly flatter and smaller, sometimes by subdividing into autonomous business units. Investment in management development activities has grown steadily. Terms and phrases associated with the human relations movement such as *empowerment, manager as coach and facilitator, teamwork,* and *leadership,* have indeed increased in popularity. As an example, at St. Francis Medical Center in Peoria, Illinois, vast changes in health care services prompted the move to 360° feedback. Personnel cuts, particularly among support staff, and delayering, or flattening the organization, changed the way employees performed their work. Employees now have more interaction with co-workers and customers, and consequently, their input has increased in value.

Despite all these changes and new terminology, most employees in most organizations still recognize the manager as boss. Like it or not, the traditional organization still rules the day. Therefore, upward appraisal can bring out the fears of employees, as well as managers. Employees may fear reprisal as a result of providing negative feedback to their managers. Assurances of confidentiality or anonymity may only go so far, especially if employees believe that company personnel, such as managers and HR specialists, have access to completed surveys. Ironically, feedback forms often break the numbers down by providing counts of responses, such as how many 1s, 2s, 3s, and so forth the manager received on a question, in such a way that managers may know—or think they know—who is providing low ratings or negative write-in comments.

On the other hand, managers may fear losing control. If a company uses 360° appraisals for evaluative purposes, managers may feel obligated to reciprocate in their own ratings of subordinates or peers. That is, to ensure high ratings from subordinates or peers in the appraisal process, the manager may feel a need to give high ratings to them. Game playing or implicit blackmail may ensue. Unfortunately, the result will not improve the effectiveness of appraisal systems. Organizational performance could also suffer because, under such circumstances, the manager will feel less authority to maintain employee accountability, thinking "If I get tough on them, they may give me low ratings."

So what does all this imply for the implementation of 360° feedback programs? Stated quite simply, 360° feedback is not the same as merely changing the rating format on a performance appraisal instrument, such as when a format shifts from agree/disagree to excellent/poor. The adoption of 360° feedback, especially upward feedback, in many organizations requires changes in organizational culture, as well as careful consideration of the dynamics of the appraisal and organizational contexts. Approaching implementation as an aspect or device for organizational change should increase the likelihood of its success. Thus, dealing with issues such as organizational resistance start to take precedence.

ORGANIZATIONAL CHANGE AND 360° FEEDBACK

Three key issues need to be addressed if the successful implementation of 360° feedback is likened to an organizational change effort. These include (1) the push-pull relationship between such feedback programs and an organization's culture, (2) the linkage with organization development, and (3) desired versus realistic outcomes.

Push-Pull

Does an organization implement 360° feedback to effect organizational change, thus stressing the *push* phenomenon? Alternatively, is an organization with a culture that already stresses change and innovation likely to engage in 360° feedback processes, thus stressing the *pull* phenomenon? Although these questions may seem academic, they are important to consider for at least two reasons.

First, the answers to these questions have direct implications for **implementation** success, that is, whether the 360° feedback program will take hold. This text will assume an organization is indeed implementing 360° feedback to effect organizational change. It will also assume the organization does not currently possess a culture stressing change and innovation, but would like to use 360° feedback as a mechanism to push the culture in that direction. As an example, Fiat has used upward feedback for precisely this purpose.[5] Taking it one step further, the text will assume the organization has engaged in other organizational change efforts in the past such as total quality implementation, but has either dropped those efforts or scaled down support dramatically. In all likelihood, some degree of employee cynicism will exist with regard to change efforts in general and 360° feedback in particular. The cynicism will be reflected in managers' pessimistic outlooks with regard to any real change that might result from the feedback. Moreover, employees may blame "those responsible" for lacking the motivation or ability to effect real change. In any event, resistance will likely appear, thus preventing a wholehearted implementation effort. This may be especially evident when it comes time to do a second wave of the program in an attempt to institutionalize 360° feedback, and survey completion rates decline dramatically.

On the other hand, an organization that already possesses a culture stressing change and innovation will likely engage in a 360° feedback process as a mere extension of that culture. That is, 360° feedback is simply seen as a tool to reinforce that culture. This reflects a *pull* phenomenon whereby the existing culture allows 360° feedback to be adopted and accepted. Employees will likely value the opportunity to provide the feedback, lack suspicion and cynicism, and generally embrace the implementation process. For example, at Xerox Human Resource Solutions in Rochester, New York, 360° feedback has simply reinforced the existing corporate culture that encourages self-directed teams and deemphasizes top-down management.

A second, obvious reason for considering the *push* and *pull* phenomena has to do with **outcome** success. This refers to enhanced managerial and organizational performance, issues embraced in detail later in this book. When the *pull* phenomenon is in play, outcome success may seem apparent. However, in reality, the culture may already support innovation and change, and the actual effects of 360° feedback are more reinforcing than instrumental.

The *push* scenario leaves more room for success directly attributable to 360° feedback. If the implementation problems mentioned above can be overcome, such feedback processes can positively impact the culture. In turn, managerial effectiveness can begin to improve significantly.

Organizational Development

The field of organizational development (OD) has grown in importance in recent years as firms struggled to engage effectively in the change processes so necessary for survival in the present environment.

Table 2-1
A Comparison of Organizational Development and
360° Feedback Implementation

Key Organizational Development Principles*	360° Feedback Implementation Strategies and Activities
Attention paid to ensuring buy-in	Top-management commitment; internal championing
Emphasis on continuous data collection and reevaluation	Action research
Active collaboration between change agents and organizational members	Frequent two-way planning and problem-solving
Freedom to contribute without fear of retribution	Anonymity of data; encouragement to use data constructively
Increases the power of all organizational members	Empowers employees rather than depowering managers
Long-term orientation and planned change	A sequence of implementation steps

* These principles have been adapted from W. L. French and C. H. Bell, Jr., *Organization Development,* 5th ed. (Englewood Cliffs, N.J.: Prentice-Hall, 1995).

OD can be defined as a top-management-supported, long-range effort to improve an organization's problem-solving and change processes, particularly through two-way collaboration and more effective management of organizational culture. Moreover, OD typically involves the assistance of a consultant-facilitator and the use of behavioral science technology, including action research.[6] Action research is a process whereby survey data are used to identify problems and solutions, and as problems get solved, new problems may become apparent. The connection between 360° feedback and organizational culture, mentioned above, will be addressed in greater detail in Chapter 5. Other aspects of OD and its linkages to 360° feedback are summarized in Table 2-1 and discussed below.

Top-Management Support. Time devoted to buy-in, or acceptance, is a fact of life in the implementation of OD and change. Organizations and the individuals who control them do not change easily, and 360° feedback represents potential change in power structures, as well as appraisal processes. Change agents, both internal and external, must gain the confidence of organizational members and take time to make the case for 360° feedback and plan implementation. This could include a series of meetings with power holders, which obviously goes beyond human resource managers to include executives, line managers, union representatives, and others.

For the most part, change agents should be external to the organization, such as consultants, especially if the organization uses 360° feedback to *push* culture change. Internal change agents may be suspected of having personal loyalties or agendas, which would not exist for external consultants. For example, they may be seen as corporate HR types who cannot be trusted with confidential information.

For now, the point is to stress the comparison between OD and 360° feedback, and how the effective implementation of the latter also tends to hinge on steps taken early to ensure organizational entry and buy-in. Managers at various hierarchical levels may distrust the 360° survey/feedback process and fear its consequences. At the same time, they may not readily speak up for fear of appearing to be unwilling to change or not to be team players. Only an ongoing, free flow of information and discussions with change agents might allay such fears.

Despite the premise regarding the importance of external change agents, the necessity of an internal champion should not be underestimated. Such an individual or group of individuals could help identify managers who might resist 360° feedback processes. Extra communication would be required with those managers. Internal champions also could attempt to smooth implementation activities.

But this does not discount the need for buy-in on the part of lower-level employees or those providing feedback. Despite having less formal power than managers, employees hold the key to moving a 360° feedback process ahead. They need to have an opportunity to voice their reservations, and they need assurance of such things as anonymity, protection from retribution, and improvements that will occur as a result of 360° feedback.

Action Research Model. OD relies on continuous data collection and reevaluation of change efforts. An action research model is commonly applied. Using such a model requires a commitment to spend time collecting data and information about problems before moving ahead with action plans. For example, if a perceived morale problem exists, a company might do an attitude survey about relevant topics, such as pay and supervision, before deciding what the problem is. After careful planning and evaluation with data at hand, the company would implement actions or programs. Then, over time, a reevaluation would occur, and new directions might be taken.

Many implementation efforts begin with a pilot study within a small portion of the overall targeted organization. Depending on the success of the pilot effort, 360° feedback could subsequently be rolled out across the greater organization. As noted later, an analysis of success in these pilot studies is typically limited to an assessment of the smoothness of implementation efforts and manager/employee reactions to the process. Pilot studies have not been used to determine actual outcome success, such as positive changes in organizational culture or performance attributable to 360° feedback. Thus, organizations often jump head first into widescale rollouts without having clear pictures of potential outcomes.

On the surface, a careful pilot study approach might sound fine to an executive wishing to implement 360° feedback. After all, to quote the old adage, "You have to learn to crawl before you can walk." However, the typical manager might develop reservations when he or she learns an outcomes-oriented pilot study may take a year or longer to complete. The need for a control group of individuals who receive no feedback may be stressed to determine if any observed positive—or negative—outcomes are indeed due to 360° feedback, as opposed to other things going on simultaneously in the organization.

Nevertheless, real-world implementations tend to discourage the use of control groups. In sum, action research can become an involved process for which some managers may not have patience, and thus, luxuries like control groups are rarely seen. The lack of a control group minimizes the extent to which a company can validly evaluate the pilot effort.

Collaboration and Two-Way Communication. The success of a 360° feedback program may hinge largely on a strategy of active collaboration with organizational members through frequent two-way planning and problem solving. To better understand exactly what this means and why it is so important, this section will consider the opposite scenario. That is, it will consider a case of little two-way communication and planning between program designers and organizational members.

An executive at XYZ Company decides upward feedback might help her organization by empowering employees and holding managers accountable for their actions toward subordinates. She contracts with a consulting firm, which administers an off-the-shelf, upward feedback survey to employees and an accompanying self-appraisal survey to managers. To the surprise of both the consultants and the executive, a low response rate occurs. As a result, few managers have sufficient data to provide reliable feedback, and the overall process is considered a failure.

How could this happen? A look at the recent history of a large telecommunication company reveals some answers. This company will be referred to as Comtel. Comtel, like many organizations, has witnessed a number of initiatives—and fads—with hopes of improving productivity, quality, or other aspects of organizational effectiveness. For example, total quality management (TQM) was implemented in the late 1980s and early 1990s. Although promising at first, the TQM initiative seemed to lose steam after a few years because it did not clearly demonstrate positive outcomes, and consequently managerial commitment faltered.

More recently, Comtel administered an employee attitude survey across a particular division of the company. The procedure involved sending surveys to employees' homes using the U.S. mail system. The surveys assured employees of confidentiality and told them they could not be identified. However, much to their surprise, employees who did not initially complete their surveys received a second survey after a few weeks. Evidently, an identifying mark on all surveys and accompanying return envelopes allowed identification of who had and had not returned surveys. As the upshot, employees became quite leery of assurances of confidentiality or anonymity.

More about Comtel follows in the next chapter. For now, one can simply note that Comtel represents a company using upward feedback in a desire to *push* the organizational culture in a positive direction. However, history provides a clear picture of why employees lacked confidence that this new upward feedback initiative would benefit Comtel. Moreover, employees lacked trust regarding how the data would be collected, stored, and processed.

Active collaboration and communication can help restore confidence and trust that has gone sour because of prior change failures or a problematic culture. Two-way communication is necessary between change agents, champions, liaisons, *and* the employees and managers who are the focus of any 360° feedback program. Several administrative issues will need to be jointly determined by all parties involved. Examples include the nature of survey questions, methods to assure confidentiality or anonymity, feedback procedures, and ultimate uses of the data. Aside from confidentiality, perhaps the most perplexing implementation issue involves whether or not the company should use 360° feedback data for evaluative purposes. Again, collaborative efforts must be taken to determine when, if ever, 360° feedback data might be used to help formally evaluate the performance of managers.

Anonymity. Another aspect of OD that corresponds with 360° feedback involves assuring anonymity to participants who provide feedback and reducing their fears of retribution. Recently research has stressed the need for anonymity in upward feedback processes.[7] OD is based largely on the notion that organizational members should feel free to contribute ideas and input without fear of retribution. To accomplish this, it is essential that (1) data collection is anonymous, and (2) data will be used for constructive purposes. The potential importance of having an external change agent controlling the process has special relevance with regard to anonymity. Participants generally feel more confident of anonymity when outsiders conduct the process, as opposed to any attempt by insiders to collect 360° feedback data.

How might 360° feedback *not* be used for constructive purposes? The authors recently learned of an organization that had utilized upward feedback to provide data to back up disciplinary procedures against targeted managers. The use of upward feedback in such an ad hoc, punitive manner not only runs counter to the spirit of OD and change but also may not be legally defensible. That is, because the data, if anonymous, cannot be traced to particular individuals, it may be difficult to prove its validity and authenticity in court.

The Issue of Power. Table 2-1 also notes another key OD principle: to increase the power of *all* members of an organization. A 360° feedback process, especially one that becomes institutionalized, does just that. Although some managers might view a 360° feedback process—especially one involving upward feedback—as a depowering experience, the opposite will occur if they learn from their feedback and thus better develop expert and referent powers. For example, a manager who, subsequent to feedback, improves his or her personal and leadership effectiveness will, at the same time, improve his or her ability to influence.

Planned Change. The possibility exists that the evaluation of a 360° feedback pilot study will reveal no significant improvements. If this occurred, one would need to determine possible reasons. A lack of improvement would signal the need for more piloting before any attempt at rollout. Assuming the pilot results are relatively favorable, the next step would be to plan a general rollout. Table 2-1 depicts OD as a long-term endeavor composed of a series of planned change steps. Likewise, the effective implementation of 360° feedback should be viewed over the long term. Indeed, the temporal distance between initial 360° feedback program planning and possible rollout may reach eighteen months.

Again, a long-term, tricky issue involves the possible use of 360° feedback for evaluative purposes. Many existing managerial appraisal forms include some weighting given to people-development issues. Indeed, people development could be viewed as perfectly suited for upward feedback input. After all, the higher-level manager conducting an appraisal often has little valid insight into how well the lower-level manager develops his or her people. Upward appraisals could provide information relevant to whether or not managers truly develop their people and groups. It would then follow that at least the portion of a manager's appraisal devoted to people development could simply be assessed on the basis of upward appraisal scores.

Unfortunately, as with other evaluative procedures, this strategy raises the possibility of political game playing and maneuvering.[8] Managers and employees may engage in implicit, or even explicit, deal making to ensure high upward appraisals. Avoiding manipulations of the system may be difficult when reciprocal evaluation occurs between boss and subordinates.

In short, the potential politics of linking upward appraisal to formal evaluation deserves at least some consideration.

On the other hand, advantages of making various forms of 360° feedback evaluative do exist. One key advantage is it may provide a means of promoting accountability. In other words, the message will be clear that the organization is serious about expecting managers to improve as a result of the feedback they receive.

Some proponents of OD might seriously question evaluative uses. The spirit of OD implies an emphasis on developing organizational effectiveness in such a manner that it simultaneously furthers the growth and security of individuals. Evaluation implies potentially threatening situations for those being evaluated. Nevertheless, performance appraisal has been considered a potentially viable tool of OD.[9] Chapter 6 will explore this issue in more detail as it considers how 360° feedback can impact individual performance.

Another long-term issue facing any general rollout of a 360° feedback program regards the length of time it should last. Some might argue that 360° feedback should be viewed like any other appraisal effort and, hence, institutionalized and conducted on a yearly basis. A counter argument maintains that, like other OD techniques, the felt need for 360° feedback may diminish over time or may be sporadic. Other techniques, such as general attitude survey feedback and teambuilding, may seem more important as an organization matures. In such an instance, perhaps only new managers and managers who transfer to new groups might receive formal 360° feedback. In short, viewing 360° feedback in a more fluid manner may place it within a larger OD system and thus help prevent the more negative status of short-term fad or flavor of the month.

Desired and Realistic Outcomes

In a recent meeting with an executive of a company attempting to implement 360° feedback, the authors asked a simple, straightforward question: "What do you hope and expect this program will accomplish for your company?" At first, the executive seemed taken aback. Then he sat back in his chair, stared at the ceiling for a moment while pondering, and finally gave an answer. Surprisingly, the answer was not altogether organized and certainly not well thought out. It included notions relevant to improved culture and managerial awareness and effectiveness. But exactly how the process might affect the firm's bottom line was certainly not clear in the mind of this executive. In fact, the executive seemed to think the authors, as experts, should be able to tell him what he could expect! To be fair, expectations also are not clear in the minds of many other executives in the business world who have, nevertheless, allocated thousands of dollars to such programs in their respective firms in recent years.

One way to understand better this lack of clarity is to consider an interesting phenomenon occurring these days that can be likened to the old adage "Keeping up with the Joneses." On more than one occasion, executives and internal change agents have shown a great deal of interest in understanding how many other firms—especially competitors—"do" 360° feedback. Indeed, these people often show more interest in other firms than in understanding desired outcomes in their own firms. Chapter 4 tells more about this phenomenon.

In the case of the above executive, the problem is that without having both desired and realistic outcomes in mind, the likelihood of reaching success becomes minimal. One likely answer to the question posed in the story above is, "Our firm wants to see improved customer satisfaction and firm performance as a result of 360° feedback." Unfortunately, the cause-and-effect is not so simple. Such simplistic thinking often results from an engineering or capital resources mentality. For example, managers may be accustomed to seeing direct, quick benefits from investments in capital resources, such as machinery. In contrast, outcomes of investments in human resources take longer to materialize. Moreover, such outcomes only likely occur by first positively impacting the firm's culture.

It is also likely that other programs or human resource initiatives will simultaneously impact the culture. For example, in addition to 360° feedback, a firm may implement new approaches toward identifying leadership talent as a part of managerial selection and promotion strategies. Thus, 360° feedback in combination with new selection and promotion standards can create a favorable impact on the culture.

In sum, if one views the implementation of 360° feedback as part of an organizational change effort, the issue of forming a clear understanding of outcomes becomes paramount in two ways. First, executives should attempt to understand clearly why they pursue 360° feedback and what they hope to accomplish. Second, they must form realistic expectations about the length of time it will take for outcomes such as cultural change to accrue, as well as what the relevant indicators of such change might look like.

SUMMARY AND CONCLUSION

This chapter has questioned the treatment of 360° feedback as a simple psychometric issue. These feedback programs represent significant organizational interventions. As such, they deserve to be viewed from an organizational change perspective, which includes understanding why organizations adopt 360° feedback. Some adopt it in the hope of *pushing* a culture toward a more open, supportive, and innovative direction. Other adoptions simply coincide with an already strong culture and, accordingly, are *pulled* along.

To view 360° feedback as in line with organizational change also causes one to draw parallels to the more established field of OD. This chapter reviewed many OD principles then compared them directly to strategies for effectively implementing 360° feedback programs. At the heart of these strategies is the idea that 360° feedback implementation should be pursued using an action research model involving continual collaboration between change agents and organizational members.

Finally, organizations pursuing 360° feedback should give careful consideration to both desired and realistic outcomes. The next chapter presents examples of strategic context and problems that must be taken into account to ensure the effective implementation of 360° feedback programs.

REFERENCES

1. For more explanation regarding high-involvement organizations, see E. E. Lawler III, *High-Involvement Management: Participative Strategies for Improving Organizational Performance* (San Francisco: Jossey-Bass, 1986).

2. Ibid.

3. For more, see P. Richards, "Right-Side-Up Organization," *Quality Progress* (October 1991), pp. 95–96.

4. For evidence regarding recipients' negative reactions to anonymous ratings, see D. Antonioni, "The Effects of Feedback Accountability on Upward Appraisal," *Personnel Psychology,* 47 (1994), pp. 349–356.

5. See E. Auteri, "Upward Feedback Leads to Culture Change," *HR Magazine* (June 1994), pp. 78–80, 82, 84.

6. This definition was taken from W. L. French and C. H. Bell, Jr., *Organization Development,* 5th ed. (Englewood Cliffs, N.J.: Prentice-Hall, 1995).

7. Antonioni, "Effects," op cit.

8. The politics and game playing associated with various types of performance appraisal is discussed in C. O. Longenecker, H. P. Sims, Jr., and D. A. Gioia, "Behind the Mask: The Politics of Employee Appraisal," *Academy of Management Executive,* 1 (1987), pp. 183–193.

9. French and Bell, op cit.

CHAPTER 3

Examples of Strategic Implementation Problems

How should an organization go about implementing 360° feedback? Answers to this question, of course, depend on the experience with and knowledge of such processes on the part of those individuals considering implementation. Regardless of experience, some common questions typically come to mind:

1. Who will the process involve?

2. Does the organization have the necessary personnel to administer the process, or should the organization employ a consulting firm?

3. How much time will survey/feedback processes require on the part of all individuals involved?

4. Can the organization use an off-the-shelf survey, or does it need to allocate employee and/or consultant time to construct its own? What types of questions should the survey ask? Should it ask open-ended questions?

5. How will 360° information be processed and then fed back to participants?

6. How will anonymity be preserved?
7. How will follow-up activities be pursued? For example, in the case of upward feedback, will targeted managers be encouraged to approach subordinates for additional feedback beyond that supplied on feedback forms?
8. How often should the organization repeat the process?
9. How will the organization encourage/reward behavior change among those receiving feedback?

All these questions are appropriate and will need consideration at some point to ensure an effective implementation. But they do not tell the entire implementation story. These particular questions are *tactical* in nature. They are intended to get at the nuts and bolts of implementation.

Most recent implementations of 360° feedback, indeed, emphasize primarily tactical issues. Some good, practical reasons for this emphasis exist. When an organization decides, for whatever reason, to pursue 360° feedback, excitement levels on the part of the planners elevate. Planners feel like they're doing something good for people and the organization. Managers also typically desire to quickly devise a plan and get it done. Of course, no one wants an inefficient or obviously flawed plan, so the questions listed above are eminently important to consider from a tactical viewpoint.

A reading of the packages provided by consulting firms suggests they have tactical emphases. Some consulting firms offer off-the-shelf 360° surveys, while others will tailor-make the survey for the needs of the organization. Some will collect the actual data, while others only process data collected by in-house staff. Moreover, feedback forms designed by consulting firms come in all sizes and shapes, with various means of displaying data for the targeted participants.

The tactical issues are obviously important to consider in any 360° feedback implementation effort. Any effort will fail if these issues are not carefully considered and monitored. For example, if anonymity is compromised, grievances and widespread mistrust of the process could result in a lack of participation. A poorly designed or confusing survey could also cause a lack of participation. As another example, poor planning could result in prohibitive and unnecessary costs.

Despite their importance, tactical implementation issues are only one set of issues organizations must address. Another set of issues pertains to strategic implementation. As described below, these issues have equal, or even more, importance than the tactical implementation issues. Yet, more often than not, they are not carefully considered or even fully understood. Consequently, from a strategic perspective, 360° implementation efforts often flounder or fail to produce desired outcomes.

Strategic issues have broader scopes than their tactical counterparts. They involve policy considerations that could have long-term effects on individual and organizational performance. To fully appreciate strategic issues and their implications, an historical perspective must place 360° feedback within the context of the organization's past. The remainder of this chapter is devoted to these issues. Specifically, the chapter will consider two key areas: (1) the controversy surrounding development versus evaluative usages of 360° feedback, and (2) the current and historical organizational backdrop of a 360° implementation effort. The chapter will also present some recent case study and interview findings relevant to these strategic areas.

SHOULD WE DEVELOP OR SHOULD WE EVALUATE?

The question of development versus evaluation is not really new. In fact, discussions have taken place for many years with regard to the general topic of performance appraisal. An emphasis on development would suggest that performance information should be collected and fed back to help individuals identify weaknesses or problems so they could make improvements. In contrast, an emphasis on evaluation would suggest organizations should use such information to make judgments and decisions about individuals, including their relative standings in the organization. In reality, both development and evaluation have been stressed in the implementation of performance appraisal systems.

However, in recent times experts have criticized the evaluative nature of performance appraisal. These criticisms stem from two main concerns. First, an emphasis on evaluation breeds game playing and manipulation in appraisal systems. Second, individual evaluation assumes that performance outcomes can be attributed to individuals. In reality, in line with the principles of total quality management, much of the variance in performance outcomes can be attributed to system-level factors beyond the control of individuals.[1]

And 360° feedback has not escaped the development versus evaluation debate. Some individuals strongly propose using 360° feedback as purely a developmental strategy to foster self-awareness and improvement. They would argue that, similar to other forms of appraisal, using 360° ratings as part of evaluation would lead to less accurate ratings. UPS questioned employees after they had provided upward ratings about whether they would have altered the ratings if they knew the company would use them as part of managers' formal performance evaluations. The findings suggested that some would raise and some would even lower ratings to affect outcomes. Second, on strictly legal grounds, organizations may find it difficult to defend negative personnel decisions such as demotion, stemming from low overall 360° appraisals. For example, in an upward feedback process, if only five out of fourteen subordinates respond to the survey, is this representative of the group and, hence, valid data for evaluation purposes? Third, the validity of using 360° information for evaluative purposes may be based on a faulty assumption—namely, that observed changes in scores over time directly result from observed changes in *real* performance. Recent research has shown that, at least to some degree, observed changes in scores over time can stem from such simple statistical artifacts as regression to the mean.[2] That is, over time high scores tend to come down closer to average and low scores tend to come up closer to average, regardless of true change. Alternatively, a lack of observed changes can indicate that observers' standards or expectations change over time, and average performance in the mind of subordinates no longer represents the same standard it did six months ago.

Other people acknowledge the importance of development but, at the same time, endorse the use of 360° feedback for evaluation. Such individuals might acknowledge the above problems but would point out that if the 360° program is to have any real teeth, it must find a way to incorporate an evaluative component. For example, they would support the notion that companies incorporate upward feedback information directly into managerial performance appraisal processes. Obviously, the precise weighting of the feedback within the appraisal compared with other information such as operational results, could vary. But the message to those receiving feedback would be clear: Score highly in terms of 360° feedback to obtain rewards and avoid punishments or disciplinary actions.

Incidentally, the debate over development versus evaluation with regard to 360° feedback has been prominent at recent meetings of the Society for Industrial and Organizational Psychology (SIOP), which include both academic and practitioner members active in the study and implementation of such feedback processes. The recent thinking appears to be that as 360°

feedback matures in organizations, pressures to include evaluative aspects will increase.

This debate over whether to include 360° ratings in evaluation is highly charged, and examples of the debate show up in the case study and interview data described later in this chapter. For now, the authors simply wish to pose a few suggestions for dealing with this sensitive strategic issue. First, quite simply, go slow. The implementation of 360° feedback represents something new for many organizations. Anything new can be potentially threatening. For example, research has shown that both upward and peer ratings garner wider acceptance when used for developmental as opposed to evaluative uses.[3] Indeed, managers have grown accustomed to being the ones who formally provide, rather than receive, feedback. At first glimpse, managers usually embrace the general concept of 360° feedback. However, the threat levels rise immediately when evaluation enters the equation. As supported by recent research, managers may be more accepting of evaluative usages over time, after receiving a chance to make developmental improvements based on earlier 360° feedback.[4]

Acceptability is increasingly being viewed as an important factor in the implementation of appraisal/feedback processes. Accordingly, the authors recommend that acceptability be a prime consideration in any adoption of a strategy emphasizing evaluation. Moreover, it seems only fair to give people 360° feedback information, let them try to improve, and then let them see if improvement has actually occurred before using the information for evaluation. That is, the survey and feedback process should complete at least two cycles. During the first cycle, ratees receive feedback, set goals, and attempt to make changes. Six months to a year later, organizations should readminister the surveys and provide ratees with feedback a second time, which allows them to see if their raters in fact noticed improvements. If an organization then wants to use 360° ratings for evaluative purposes, the targeted individuals will at least have familiarized themselves with the process and know where they stand.

A second suggestion involves not taking the rating scores so literally, as if measuring with a yardstick. For example, in an upward feedback process, scores among an organization's managers might average 3.8 on a 1-to-5 scale, where 5 represents the highest possible score. Should a score of 4.2 be considered better than a score of 4.0? When exactly should one begin to consider scores significantly different? In light of the rating problems mentioned above, making fine distinctions between ratings can present problems, especially when everybody knows the company uses ratings for evaluation.

Accordingly, a simple approach should be taken. In most any rating process, it is not too difficult to distinguish the superstars from the developmentally challenged. The same rings true with regard to 360° ratings. For example, in an upward appraisal process, anyone scoring more than two standard deviations below the mean—especially twice in a row—obviously has problems in his or her role, which warrant some type of evaluative or developmental action. Likewise, anyone scoring substantially above the mean may deserve special credit. The problem arises when companies make evaluative judgments about, and actions are taken toward, people in the middle of the distribution.

In sum, *strategic* as well as tactical decisions are necessary to determine how 360° feedback information will be used. The authors propose a go-slow, cautionary policy with regard to using 360° feedback for evaluative purposes. Now attention turns to the broader strategic issues surrounding the current and historical organizational backdrop of a 360° implementation effort.

PLACING 360° FEEDBACK WITHIN AN ORGANIZATIONAL CONTEXT

The implementation of a 360° feedback program represents an initiative hopefully designed to improve human resources and organizational communication. When attempting to understand the real impact of such programs, one should not examine them independently of their organizational contexts. From a temporal perspective, two aspects of the context act as keys to this understanding: (1) the present, and (2) the past.

The Present

In an organization's present, other strategies in the form of events, programs, policies, or initiatives may occur simultaneously to 360° feedback. In other words, it does not occur in a vacuum. A 360° initiative may be intentionally linked to other organizational strategies or, alternatively, may simply be occurring fortuitously at the same time. Either way, organizational members will draw linkages, and interactive effects will occur.

Downsizing. For example, the recent trend toward organizational downsizing could occur either intentionally or unintentionally at the same time as the initiation of 360° feedback. In general, a 360° feedback implementation should be compatible with other business strategies. Downsizing accompanied by 360° feedback efforts creates strange bedfellows. Employees may fear that the real purpose of collecting 360° ratings is to have data to help decide who to cut. Such a context does not facilitate accurate and honest ratings and may indeed be destructive.

Reward Systems. An additional strategic issue concerns the organization's reward systems and the extent to which they reinforce the practices encouraged by the feedback process. For example, an upward feedback survey may identify behaviors necessary to effectively manage and develop subordinates. However, if the organization's reward system merely rewards bottom-line, short-term results, regardless of how those results are achieved, the survey and feedback will serve no useful purpose. Consequently, it is critical to measure what the organization truly wants to encourage. This may require the organization to develop a tailor-made survey, emphasizing behaviors and values the organization most wants to encourage. It may also require a reconsideration of managerial performance appraisal criteria, that is, appraisal criteria may need alignment with the criteria being emphasized in the 360° feedback process.

Additionally, it is important to recognize that if the upward feedback instrument encourages behaviors not previously rewarded but that will be rewarded in the future, some old behaviors may be replaced with new ones. For example, one large high-tech company is implementing a 360° feedback process requiring all supervisors to spend at least one hour per quarter with each of his or her subordinates, discussing job-relevant issues. The company did not anticipate that some supervisors have more than 50, and sometimes more than 100, subordinates. Because the supervisors cannot actually add 50 or 100 hours to the quarter, this translates into a number of hours that will require different allocation than in the past. Is the organization willing to specify what things supervisors can stop doing to embrace the new things they must do?

Globalization. Globalization strategies are largely compatible with efforts toward 360° feedback. As organizations attempt to globalize the production and marketing of their products or services, communication between increasingly diverse individuals becomes inherent. When increased communication becomes necessary, so too will the potential for miscommunication between people with diverse cultural backgrounds. For example, Honeywell's engineering operations in Phoenix include people from a host of different nationalities. Team-based structures at Honeywell can improve cooperation and performance, but at the same time, special challenges exist for multicultural teams attempting to be effective. Obviously, 360° feedback can act as a powerful mechanism for clarifying the miscommunication that may accrue as a result of such multiculturalism and globalization. Managers must be aware, however, that those from different cultures may receive the 360° initiative and ratings from bosses and peers differently, and therefore managers must approach them with sensitivity. For example, in collectivist cultures, such as the Japanese culture, rating individuals rather than groups is very uncommon. Asking Japanese workers to rate their supervisors may be uncomfortable for them. Additionally, in Germany individuals tend to be modest and self-deprecating when rating themselves. The inflation of self-ratings is uncommon. How will organizations manage these cultural rating style differences?

Quality Improvement. Perhaps the most compatible strategy that could occur simultaneously to 360° feedback would be quality improvement. A host of names and acronyms have been attached to quality improvement initiatives during the past ten years, such as TQM and continuous quality improvement (CQI). Some elements common to such initiatives include:

1. Closer contact with customers, both inside and outside the firm, to better meet their requirements;

2. Employee empowerment to provide input toward and take responsibility for decisions;

3. An organization that communicates more openly;

4. The development and rewarding of leadership behavior;

5. The use of measurement to better plan and set goals; and

6. Team-based structure.

This list is not intended to exhaust all the elements that have characterized quality improvement initiatives.[5] However, it does capture elements particularly in line with 360° feedback. A strong customer-supplier relationship norm (see above, list item 1) provides the basis for accepting formalized customer feedback to suppliers. Customers could include external individuals, internal peers, and even subordinates.

Employee empowerment (list item 2), coupled with an organization designed to communicate more freely and openly (list item 3), also provides compatibility with a 360° initiative. The 360° feedback becomes a mechanism to show employees they truly are empowered to freely communicate whether needs and expectations are being met by their internal "suppliers," that is, peers and managers. Some employees, or "customers," might argue that the empowerment is not complete unless their feedback ultimately gets used for evaluative purposes concerning their internal suppliers. Some research has shown that customers favor input into evaluation more than the suppliers they rate do.[6]

It may be a cliché to suggest leadership (list item 4) is an essential ingredient of quality improvement processes. Beginning with the pioneers of the quality revolution, individuals such as W. Edwards Deming and Joseph Juran have repeatedly suggested the importance of leadership for the achievement of significant organizational advances in quality.[7] Since its inception, the Malcolm Baldrige National Quality Award has clearly designated leadership as a key driver in making sure quality improvement truly comes about. Indeed, over the years, leadership has remained the first category of the Baldrige Award.

A closer look at the Baldrige Award reveals some interesting insights about how leadership gets defined in relation to quality improvement. For example, the leadership section begins with a focus on senior executives and their espousing of quality-oriented values and vision. It further suggests that senior executives should be personally involved in quality efforts. Perhaps even more relevant to 360° feedback, the Baldrige guidelines continue with the subcategory of Leadership System and Organization, which deals essentially with the diffusion of leadership throughout an organization. That is, an expectation is established that leadership practices should spread throughout the managerial ranks.

And 360° feedback provides an important mechanism to ensure this diffusion materializes and gets reinforced. As outlined in more detail in Chapter 6, a key to leadership effectiveness is self-awareness. When managers receive feedback about leadership weaknesses they do not know they have, many will be motivated to improve. Moreover, the feedback will recognize and reinforce leadership strengths. In short, 360° feedback provides information that fosters self-awareness, a critical element in the diffusion of leadership throughout an organization that must accompany quality improvement strategies.

Quality improvement stresses the use of measurement to plan and set goals (list item 5). Measurement helps pinpoint problems and opportunities for continuous improvement. A classic example is the use of statistical process control to analyze and improve operations. Similarly, 360° feedback provides systematically measured information that a company can use to plan and set development improvement goals. Managers can examine 360° feedback measures to pinpoint areas that need development so they can set specific goals.

Finally, increasingly, organizations are turning to team-based structures (list item 6) to improve efficiency and quality in organizations. Often these teams manage themselves by controlling their own hiring, goal setting, and budgets. These teams also often involve multiple functions across the organization, as well as multiple customers. As such, traditional top-down appraisal in itself cannot evaluate all relevant aspects of a team member's performance. More perspectives, in other words a 360° perspective, would help. In attempts to evaluate individual team members, input from peers or team members, customers, and perhaps other teams would prove helpful in addition to input from functional managers and/or project managers.

Summary. This section has presented four key strategies that may occur in the *present* context simultaneously to the initiation of 360° feedback: downsizing, reward systems, globalization, and quality improvement. These strategies may be intentionally linked to 360° feedback or, alternatively, may simply occur by chance. Either way, organizational members will draw linkages, and the various initiatives, including 360° feedback, will interact with each other. The interaction will be negative for downsizing strategies but positive for globalization and quality improvement. In addition, reward systems must properly align with 360° feedback processes. Now attention turns to the *past* organizational context to introduce an historical perspective that should be taken into account during the implementation of 360° feedback.

The Past

Managerial actions and initiatives that occur in the present cannot be separated from those that occurred in the past—at least not in the minds of organizational members who stand to be affected. In other words, people tend to remember—and stories will be told to new employees about—actions and initiatives that occurred in the past. The extent to which a 360° feedback initiative succeeds may hinge on the favorableness of past memories.

During the past thirty years, organizations have witnessed a wide gamut of initiatives spearheaded by management. These include organizationally focused change efforts such as management-by-objectives, team-based work design, quality circles, total quality management, and reengineering. They also include change efforts focused more on jobs and human resources, such as job enrichment, gainsharing, and quality of worklife programs. Many of these initiatives have shown positive results, although at times, the results have been less than spectacular.

A phenomenon may be developing in many organizations whereby individuals have grown cynical about such change initiatives.[8] This cynicism develops based on at least two key factors. First, organizational members observe that management initiates an organizational change strategy, such as a quality improvement program. The new direction may appear to be a knee-jerk reaction to some problem, such as turnover, sudden lack of productivity, increased competition, or an attempt to copy other firms' actions. Subsequently, after the initial excitement and hoopla wear off, it becomes apparent that other priorities or day-to-day pressures have come to the forefront, and commitment to the change strategy has begun to waver. Some mistakes, such as lack of care taken to ensure anonymity in a survey process and unavailability of necessary training, could occur in the implementation process, leaving a bad taste in the mouths of organizational members.

Second, because of the wavering commitment, little return on investment is realized, and management undertakes another knee-jerk reaction whereby the initiative is watered down, cancelled, or put on hold. This scenario could be accentuated by a replacement of the top management team, whereby the new team either does not approve of the original change strategy or simply desires to initiate its own pet program(s).

What would all this have to do with a present-day attempt to implement 360° feedback? Unfortunately, individuals' memories are not short, and often employees remain with the organization much longer than top managers. The failure to appropriately or fully implement prior initiatives creates a pessimistic or cynical viewpoint with regard to new initiatives. Managers who pushed prior organizational actions appear incompetent, lacking in personal commitment, or both. Past implementation failures take on a self-fulfilling prophecy. That is, a feeling likely exists in the organization that any new initiatives, such as 360° feedback, will probably also result in major problems or will not be followed through.

In summary, the lesson here is that an organization should carefully consider any new initiatives, like 360° feedback, in light of past initiatives and change efforts. This does not suggest that previous problems and the resulting organizational cynicism that has accrued should necessarily prevent an organization from attempting to implement 360° feedback. However, past events and actions do form an important strategic context relevant to the implementation of new initiatives, and companies must take this context into account.

One way to assess the lingering damage from the past and its possible effects on the present is to heavily involve organizational members in the design of the 360° feedback process. Lingering resentments will likely surface and, thus, can be addressed. Moreover, involving people in the design and truly committing to the effort over the long run will likely alleviate resistance toward supporting the 360° feedback process. One way to show commitment is to ensure that the rating and feedback processes will *at least* complete two cycles. An example of such involvement is illustrated below.

A CASE EXAMPLE OF STRATEGIC IMPLEMENTATION PROBLEMS

Now attention turns to a case example of a 360° feedback implementation specifically emphasizing upward feedback. The case involved a firm in the telecommunication industry worldwide, although most operations were located in North America. Although operations include both production- and service-based facilities, this case focuses on a service division. That division engineered the design of telecommunication systems, installed such systems, and provided customer support.

The implementation began as a pilot project involving approximately 15 percent of the ultimately targeted managers, representing different levels of management in the service division. The purpose of the pilot was to design a suitable instrument and feedback report, to allow for input from organizational members in designing the process (primarily to ensure buy-in), to determine the potential feasibility of evaluative usages of upward feedback, and to provide some preliminary evidence of the effectiveness of upward feedback in the organization.

In light of the previous discussion of strategic issues, some interesting events surfaced during the course of this pilot study. The first centered on some higher-level managers' desires to make the upward feedback immediately evaluative. That is, they wanted to make sure lower-level managers immediately incorporated upward feedback data into the managerial performance appraisal system. Because of the inherent problems in making 360° feedback evaluative, the authors succeeded in preventing this policy from coming to fruition. Instead, as part of the eventual rollout across the division that occurred several months later, all managers were encouraged to use the upward feedback to identify developmental needs. Managers could also use the feedback data as evidence of positive change if they so chose. With the help of their higher-level supervisors, as part of the yearly performance planning process, managers were then to set developmental goals based on the feedback.

In reality, separating developmental and evaluative uses of feedback proved difficult in this organization, as well as in others that encourage ratees to share feedback and goals with their supervisors. When supervisors become aware of their subordinates' weaknesses, they often find it difficult to discount this information at appraisal time. In the case example, the managers had the option of using their feedback data as evidence of positive change. If they chose to do this, they had to share the first feedback results and compare them to a later set of feedback results to demonstrate positive change. Managers then used this positive change as part of the person's evaluation. In essence, in this organization, managers could decide whether or not to use the information as input to their appraisals. Also, in the organizational context, one third of each manager's performance appraisal was based on people development, a dimension akin to many leadership behaviors included in the upward survey. Thus, given this preexisting alignment of the current appraisal/reward system with the upward feedback process, most managers felt pressured to include the feedback results into their appraisals.

Some other interesting events took place in the organization's strategic context during and prior to the pilot project and subsequent rollout. During these events, the division underwent widespread reorganization and some downsizing. This affected the upward feedback implementation in two key ways. First, at a tactical level, determining who should provide feedback to whom became difficult. Second, the downsizing made some managers skeptical of the true purpose of the upward feedback. That is, they feared the company really intended to use upward feedback to downsize the managerial workforce. This fear was reinforced by some managers' early desire to make the feedback evaluative, as described above.

In the recent past, the organization had attempted to implement TQM. Indeed, the organization had generated much initial excitement for the principles of TQM and had undertaken some early projects.

Approximately two years before the initiation of the upward feedback pilot project, a change of CEO and portions of the top-management team occurred. With those changes came the eventual dissolving of the TQM initiative and concomitant skepticism about the longevity of any new initiative.

Another event in the organization's recent past also warrants mentioning. Only several months before the upward feedback pilot project, an external consulting agency conducted an attitude survey, described earlier. Respondents received assurances of anonymity; however, a semi-invisible computerized marking system associated all outgoing surveys with employees, so they could, in reality, be identified. Accordingly, employees who did not return their initial surveys received another survey a few weeks later. Not surprisingly, this created a large uproar among some employees who wondered how they could be identified in this "anonymous" survey process. An explanation was provided that the consulting firm used its identification system only to ensure the completion of as many surveys as possible, not to identify individual survey respondents or to report any individual's attitudes to company management. Despite these assurances, many employees remained leery of survey processes.

In sum, three current and prior events came together to provide an important strategic context to this case study of upward feedback implementation. These included concurrent reorganization and downsizing efforts, a previous effort to implement TQM that appeared prematurely abandoned, and a general attitude survey with suspicious respondent identification procedures. The net effect of this context was that it provided a less than favorable atmosphere for the implementation of upward feedback. Managers and employees alike felt either worried or ambivalent about the process for several reasons. First, managers feared how the upward feedback data would eventually be used, that is, whether it would assist downsizing decisions. Second, many felt that, like the TQM initiative, a lack of commitment for upward feedback would surface, and it would turn out to be a smoke-and-mirrors exercise. Thus, why get excited and expend a high degree of psychological energy? Third, employees—or raters in the upward feedback process—had concerns that, despite assurances of anonymity, they had no guarantees that responses would not be traced. Even if the consultants could be trusted, targeted managers could probably find some way to identify employees providing feedback, such as through written comments.

Unfortunately, many of these contextual issues were discovered after the initiation of the pilot project and during some key implementation phases. More ideally, they might have been identified in the early planning phases. Nevertheless, participatory mechanisms built into the implementation process proved helpful in discovering and attempting to deal with potentially negative aspects of the context. For example, a steering committee composed of a sample of both managers and employees was formed to work with the consultants in the planning and administration of both survey and feedback processes. Prior to actual surveying, a larger group of participants aired their inputs and concerns in a series of information sessions regarding upward feedback processes, administered by a key contact person from the firm and one of the consultants. At these sessions, the concurrent and prior contextual problems clearly surfaced. Although the information sessions did not ensure buy-in on the part of all potential participants, these sessions at least helped create a dialogue regarding current and past events that related to any new attempts to implement upward feedback. Without the information sessions, the likely outcomes would have been low response rates, little developmental goal setting, and little managerial development. Moreover, management would have had less awareness of the linkages formed among various change initiatives, and the unfortunate possibility for organizational cynicism to evolve.

As it turned out, the rollout proved quite successful for the following reasons. First, the consultants identified and helped resolve salient issues in information sessions before administering any surveys. The survey response rate exceeded 80 percent. Second, the managers involved in the pilot project spoke highly of the integrity of the process, as well as the value of the information they received. Third, managers could choose whether they wanted their feedback scores included in their appraisals. This helped in that, because of reorganization actions, many supervisors had new or challenging groups and did not feel comfortable using feedback from their groups for evaluation. Still others likely felt worried about low scores and did not want to incorporate their scores into appraisal processes until they had had the chance to improve. Fourth, the feedback accompanied other HR interventions targeted at development, such as training in giving and receiving feedback. All in all, the process succeeded, and the organization continued the process and expanded it to other divisions.

AN INTERVIEW INVESTIGATION OF STRATEGIC IMPLEMENTATION PROBLEMS

The authors recently conducted interviews with six individuals who have experience in the implementation of 360° feedback. Three of these individuals can be considered internal consultants in that they work for large corporations and design various HR programs. The corporations include a large courier service, a large oil company, and a high-tech computer firm. The other three individuals were external consultants, one of whom worked for a consulting firm actively involved in the design and implementation of 360° feedback programs for firms. The other two external consultants conducted their own private businesses. Thus, these individuals held different roles with regard to 360° feedback and its design and implementation.

The interviewers asked these six individuals a variety of questions dealing with both tactical and strategic issues that they had faced in implementation efforts. Some examples include:

1. How had they been involved in implementing upward or 360° feedback processes?

2. Were these processes designed to be used for developmental or evaluative purposes or both?

3. How were they able to assure confidentiality/anonymity? Did employees and/or managers express any fears about anonymity or possible retribution?

4. How did they evaluate the effectiveness of the 360° feedback program(s)?

5. Did the organization(s) institutionalize the program, or was it a one-time process?

6. Did they observe any game playing, manipulations, or politics regarding the process?

7. Did they have any anecdotes or lessons learned that they could share?

Below, findings of the interviews that are applicable to the strategic issues presented in this chapter have been summarized.

Although the interviewees came from different backgrounds and roles, they shared a common perspective on the issue of development versus evaluation. Almost uniformly they favored developmental usages and expressed leeriness about evaluation. Common concerns included: that evaluation would result in game playing; that it might not be fair to certain managers, such as managers whose subordinates are particularly difficult; and that potential legal fallout could result. For example, with regard to game playing, the individual representing the courier service asked some raters if their ratings would have varied if they knew those ratings would be used for evaluative purposes. Many acknowledged that yes, their ratings would have varied. Some would have rated managers higher, perhaps for fear of retribution; others would have rated lower as a means of getting back at their managers. These findings are in line with other research.[9] The individual representing an external consulting firm went so far to say that his/her firm would not sell its 360° feedback instruments or services to a company if that company planned to use it for anything but development.

Not all the interviewees were quite so adamant. One of the private external consultants commented that it only seems fair to give targeted managers some time to get familiar with the process and to try to make improvements before allowing evaluation processes to kick in. He or she then seemed to indicate that some use of evaluation might be warranted. The individual representing the courier service noted that he/she was familiar with a competitor that had, indeed, incorporated 360° feedback into the formal appraisal system. Specifically, the competitor had established a cutoff score for supervisors on its 360° instrument. If a supervisor scored below the cutoff on two consecutive survey administrations, he/she would be demoted from that supervisory position. Finally, the individual representing the high-tech computer company noted that although his/her company's program existed primarily for developmental purposes, an individual's higher-level boss also received that individual's feedback. Accordingly, the higher-level boss could incorporate the feedback into that individual's appraisal. However, our interviewee also quickly added that because of the cultural context of the company, most individuals readily accepted the process. More will be said about this below.

Most of the interviewees focused on tactical issues and concerns. However, they did explore other interesting areas. For example, interviewees commonly acknowledged that more effort should be spent figuring out exactly what the organization expects to accomplish through 360° feedback processes and then measuring those effects. As one of the private external consultants pointed out, one should not only look at individual development but also at "how the organization develops."

A few of the interviewees also recognized that the larger context of the organization needs to be taken into account to help ensure implementation effectiveness. The individual from the consulting firm noted, "Companies must recognize that the correct climate is needed for 360° feedback to work." Along these lines, a common theme was that our interviewees had not witnessed enough follow-up to 360° feedback efforts. For example, 360° feedback rarely accompanied developmental planning or formal follow-up sessions with those providing the ratings. Likewise, unlike the case example above, the interviewees tended to note little connection between the dimensions being measured as part of 360° feedback, on the one hand, and those dimensions or criteria included in the ongoing performance appraisal system, on the other.

As an interesting example, the individual at the high-tech computer company stated that to truly understand a 360° feedback implementation effort, one has "to look at the context." He/she noted that the company seemed characterized by a trusting culture, largely because of a consistent string of positive HR and quality improvement initiatives in the past. For example, when the authors interviewed this individual, his/her company already had entered its fourth year of implementation. It had been successfully pilot-tested prior to implementation in close cooperation with managers and employees. An interesting aspect of the company's process is that each targeted manager is assigned a coach to help interpret the feedback and set developmental goals. Coaches could be external consultants, internal HR people, or higher-level managers. The coaching aspect of the process demonstrated that the company truly took interest in helping managers improve.

On the other hand, as mentioned above, higher-level managers could incorporate upward feedback data into performance appraisals of targeted managers. Our interviewee noted that within the existing culture, it had become common for employees to give input to higher-level managers about their respective supervisors. In other words, the company had encouraged an open-door policy whereby employees could appropriately go to higher-level managers if they could not reconcile problems with their bosses. When formalized upward feedback processes began to evolve, it seemed perfectly normal to have the information sent not only to the targeted managers but also to their bosses. In turn, the higher-level managers could use this information for evaluative purposes. In sum, the organization had set norms for making 360° feedback information available to higher-level managers. Moreover, trust developed in the culture, whereby raters largely did not fear retribution, and managers or ratees received assurance that even if the data were used evaluatively, they would ultimately receive fair treatment. Under such contextual circumstances, using 360° feedback in evaluation seems more likely to succeed.

CONCLUSIONS

This chapter has clarified several of the more important strategic issues facing the effective implementation of 360° feedback. These issues go beyond the nuts-and-bolts tactical considerations, which, while certainly important, do not account for the entire implementation picture. Strategic issues addressed here include developmental versus evaluative purposes, present organizational context and concurrent management initiatives, and past organizational context and the possibility of built-up cynicism. To clarify these issues, a case study example was presented, as were the results of six interviews with 360° feedback practitioners.

Chapter 4 begins a new section that asks a series of strategic questions to better understand the possible impact of 360° feedback on organizations. Specifically, attention will focus on the apparent, as well as the not so obvious, reasons why an organization may choose to engage in the implementation of formalized 360° feedback.

REFERENCES

1. For more information about these appraisal issues, see the following:
   D. A. Waldman, "Designing Performance Management Systems for Total Quality Implementation," *Journal of Organizational Change Management,* 7(2) (1994), pp. 31–44.
   D. A. Waldman, "The Contributions of Total Quality Management to a Theory of Work Performance," *Academy of Management Review,* 19 (1994), pp. 510–536.
2. See J. W. Smither, et al., "An Examination of the Effects of an Upward Feedback Program Over Time," *Personnel Psychology,* 48 (1995), pp. 1–33.
3. See:
   M. London and A. Wohlers, "Agreement Between Subordinate and Self Ratings in Upward Feedback," *Personnel Psychology,* 44 (1991), pp. 375–390.
   G. M. McEvoy and P. F. Buller, "User Acceptance of Peer Appraisals in an Industrial Setting," *Personnel Psychology,* 40 (1987), pp. 785–797.

4. See D. A. Waldman, et al., "Attitudinal and Behavioral Outcomes of an Upward Feedback Process," (paper presented at the meeting of the Academy of Management, Cincinnati, August 1996).

5. For a more complete listing of elements associated with quality improvement, see:

T. C. Powell, "Total Quality Management as Competitive Advantage: A Review and Empirical Study," *Strategic Management Journal,* 16 (1995), pp. 15–37.

Waldman, "Contributions," op cit.

6. See D. Antonioni, "The Effects of Feedback Accountability on Upward Appraisal," *Personnel Psychology,* 47 (1994), pp. 349–356.

7. See:

W. E. Deming, *Out of the Crisis* (Cambridge, Mass.: Center for Advanced Engineering Study, Massachusetts Institute of Technology, 1986).

J. M. Juran, *Juran on Leadership for Quality: An Executive Handbook* (Wilson, Conn.: Juran Institute Inc., 1986).

8. The concept of organizational cynicism was presented by P. Brandes-Duncan and J.W. Dean, Jr., "An Exploration of Organizational Cynicism," (presentation given at the Academy of Management convention in Vancouver, British Columbia, Canada, August 1995).

9. See:

Antonioni, op cit.

London and Wohlers, op

CHAPTER 4

Why Do Organizations Implement 360° Feedback?

Many of the problems and risks associated with 360° feedback can be alleviated by carefully addressing the question of why organizations implement such programs. Unfortunately, companies devote more time to generating enthusiasm and making operational plans for a 360° initiative than to carefully and critically thinking about *what* they can realistically accomplish. The birth of a 360° initiative can typically be characterized as a snowball championing process. That is, an individual manager learns about the concept by receiving 360° feedback as part of a training program he or she attends, or hears about it through colleagues, readings, and so forth. That person could be an executive, a general manager, or a human resource manager. He or she champions the idea by discussing it with fellow managers. If the idea begins to build support and snowballs, the company will likely make plans to implement a formal program. As mentioned in previous chapters, these plans will include identifying targeted employees, deciding whether or not to use consultants, and developing potential timetables for surveying and feedback. One likely scenario follows.[1]

A TYPICAL CASE

A CEO from a large manufacturing company attended an executive development conference and heard about other organizations' 360° feedback programs. He liked the idea. At the conference he heard all about the potential benefits of 360° feedback. He persuaded his senior management that the company should pursue 360° feedback because it could quickly become a substitute for their current annual performance appraisal. He stated, "Three hundred sixty–degree feedback comes directly from people who are in the best positions to evaluate the performance of the people they work with. Supervisors will have more information to support their own appraisals of others and, therefore, more leverage to do something about some people's performance. We'll use the 360° feedback to help determine people's merit raises. That way, we'll make sure that people make improvements based on the feedback they received." The CEO asked the human resource management (HRM) department in the company to recruit a consulting firm that specialized in 360° feedback. HRM found a firm and then helped customize the firm's ninety-nine item, canned 360° survey. After the first round of 360° surveys, almost everyone in the organization, including the CEO, felt frustrated or disappointed with the outcomes of the process. People complained about how many surveys they had to fill out and how long the process took. In addition, since word had gotten around about the ultimate evaluative uses of 360° feedback, supervisors felt that many of the 360° ratings were inflated. Rumors had even circulated about implicit and even explicit deal making regarding ratings: "If you scratch my back by providing high ratings, I'll scratch your back in return." In short, the data had little value. The company was faced with a decision of whether to continue or discontinue the 360° feedback program. What should the organization do? What should it have done at the beginning of the process?

This case represents a typical experience for many organizations seeking to implement change initiatives, including 360° feedback programs. Word-of-mouth generates excitement. Individuals from other organizations tell stories. People make comparisons and weigh the chances of success in their own organizations. Typically left out of the planning and decision-making processes is a clear consideration of precisely what goals the organization hopes to accomplish through 360° feedback and how the organization will determine whether it has accomplished those goals. Now attention turns to providing a clear delineation of the reasons so many organizations have pursued 360° feedback in recent years. The chapter will conclude with specific recommendations that can help organizations get the most out of such programs and realize benefits rather than disappointments.

THE RATIONAL SIDE OF 360° FEEDBACK

So what is all the fuss currently about? Why do organizations invest so much effort—and money—into 360° feedback programs? Why did the CEO described above feel so anxious to adopt this process? A thoughtful analysis suggests a number of rational and logical reasons driving the current movement. However, such an analysis also identifies some less rational and potentially wasteful or hazardous reasons. First, attention turns to the more rational side of 360° feedback.

One of the key purposes driving the present 360° feedback craze involves the desire to further the cause of management or leadership development. The rationale behind this developmental goal is that providing feedback to managers about how subordinates, peers, or customers/clients view them should prompt behavior changes. In essence, many managers, and others, have not received as much honest feedback as necessary for an accurate self-perception. When a company solicits anonymous feedback from others and self-evaluations from managers, the comparison of selves and other data should allow managers to form more realistic pictures of their strengths and weaknesses.

This dose of others' perceptions would be expected to prompt behavior change in areas where weaknesses previously unknown to the managers might have been identified. Or managers might feel motivated to improve to more closely align others' perceptions with the more positive views the managers hold of themselves. Thus, behavior change would be most likely when the feedback received is negative or unexpected. However, 360° feedback can also serve a purpose by reinforcing managers for their strengths. The issue of how 360° feedback impacts individual performance will be considered in more detail in the next chapter.

Related to the goal of furthering management or leadership develop-ment, many other potential benefits are being touted. Most ultimately target organizational change and improvement. As such, 360° initiatives reflect resource dependence theory, which views organizational change as a rational response to environmental pressures for change or strategic adaptation.[2] The basic idea is that by increasing managerial self-awareness through formalized 360° or upward feedback, an organiza-tion's culture will become more participative and will be able to react more quickly to the needs of internal and external customers. This should ultimately lead to increasing levels of trust and communication between managers and their constituents, fewer grievances, and greater customer satisfaction.

A logical question is: Does it really work? Are organizations that have implemented 360° feedback programs actually accomplishing the above goals? Unfortunately, nobody really knows. With few exceptions, most research attention has focused more on the hows than the whys or whats of these programs. That is, attention has focused on how to imple-ment such a program rather than on why organizations do it or what they actually accomplish. Before turning attention to ways of remedying this sit-uation, it may be informative to look at some less rational and possibly even hazardous reasons why some organizations have pursued formalized 360° feedback.

THE LESS RATIONAL SIDE OF 360° FEEDBACK

Despite all the rational and seemingly logical reasons for pursuing a 360° feedback program that are mentioned above, at least two other less rational reasons account for its proliferation. The first has to do with a concept known as institutional theory. In essence, this theory suggests that organizations try to imitate their competition or other companies in an organizational network, such as customer companies.[3] Like resource dependence theory, institutional theory suggests that the choice to adopt 360° feedback reflects a response to pressures in a company's business environment. However, unlike resource dependence, institutional theory emphasizes conformity toward and imitation of outside companies as a driving reason for 360° feedback adoption. Such conformity gives a com-pany a sense of external legitimacy. Incidentally, in suggesting that such reasons for implementing 360° feedback may be less rational than those given earlier, perhaps it is more fair to say they are simply less performance-driven, and at least some rationality may exist in wanting to achieve legitimacy within an industry or institution.

This concept of external legitimacy is best illustrated by an example. Recently, the authors worked closely with a large company in its attempt to implement an upward feedback program. From the beginning, the authors sought to determine the precise reasons why the company wanted to pursue this program. After all, by forming a better understanding of its goals, the authors stood a better chance of serving its precise needs. It also helps in achieving buy-in if managers and employees can clearly see the goals the process intends to accomplish. While pursing this question in detail, individuals in charge of implementation, indeed, did raise some of the more rational reasons mentioned above. However, another consistent theme simply seemed to be a desire to keep up with the Joneses. That is, they persistently asked what other companies, especially companies in their industry, were doing in the way of upward feedback. They also asked for lists of other companies using upward feedback, almost as if this alone provided reason enough to adopt it.

Interestingly, a similar phenomenon of imitation occurred years ago regarding quality circles and seems to occur in organizations today regarding teams. Some organizations have created teams because the competition has them; because competitors adopted them, managers believed teams must increase efficiency or have some other positive effect. Little thought went into determining just what teams should improve or how technical and managerial systems in particular organizations would need to change to support them. That is, teams may not best accomplish the work that needs to be done, and organizations may not have the correct systems in place for teams to succeed. Yet they seem like a good idea.

For example, companies with strong merit or individualized piece-rate incentive systems will likely run counter to team thinking and behaviors. Merely creating teams will not change the ways individuals interact with one another. If reward systems stress individual competition, team members will continue to compete with one another rather than work cooperatively. In other words, "It's the reward system, stupid!"[4]

Institutional theory becomes more and more relevant as organizations face uncertain situations wherein the means of achieving desired outcomes are not altogether clear. Indeed, this may be the case for 360° feedback since little research evidence exists regarding the precise methods and contexts that allow it to positively affect organizational outcomes. In such situations, attempting to copy the actions of reputable others seems like a reasonable path to take, and later adopters, or companies adopting 360° feedback several years after it became popular, may not even question the potential effectiveness of 360° feedback. In short, this text does not argue against benchmarking other companies' actions with regard to 360° feedback initiatives. However, to benchmark without clearly understanding what a company rationally expects to gain or what it has already realized from other management initiatives seems to miss the point.

A second, potentially hazardous reason for the proliferation of 360° feedback involves the desire to make such feedback evaluative by linking it directly with a manager's or employee's formal performance appraisal. This issue, raised in the last chapter, deserves further attention here. The authors' most recent experiences suggest the pressure to make 360° feedback evaluative in nature is on the rise. Companies tend to want to use the ratings for evaluation because they believe more raters make for better appraisals, and they want to get their money's worth from the 360° process. One might question whether they get *less* for their money when they use ratings for evaluation as opposed to when they do not. Nevertheless, companies recently using subordinate input as part of the managerial appraisal process include Amoco, DuPont, Wells Fargo, Exxon, Tenneco, Johnson & Johnson, and GTE.[5]

In theory, the use of 360° feedback for evaluative purposes seems logical. If an organization holds an individual directly accountable for ratings received, he or she will have more motivation to make improvements based on the feedback. Also, the more sources of ratings, the greater the chances that biases will counterbalance each other, making ratings more reliable. Unfortunately, problems exist that may negate the possible benefits of 360° feedback if it is made evaluative. In fact, seven of fifteen companies that are part of an upward feedback consortium that had used 360° feedback for appraisal have stopped. They ceased their use of appraisal largely because of employees' negative attitudes and inflated ratings that were not useful for making decisions about employees.[6]

Another problem in using 360° feedback ratings for evaluation purposes is that research has demonstrated that when ratings become evaluative rather than purely developmental, up to 40 percent of raters change their ratings. In some cases the ratings go up, and in some they go down, but nevertheless, they become less useful for development because raters modify them to affect outcomes. As previously mentioned, UPS tested the potential of using 360° feedback ratings for evaluation by questioning employees after they had provided upward ratings. UPS asked employees whether they would have altered the ratings if they knew the information would be used in managers' formal performance evaluations. Some individuals said they would raise ratings, and some even said they would lower them in such a case. Employees would change these ratings primarily to affect outcomes, such as to keep their managers from trouble or in some cases to get their managers in trouble.

Relatedly, 360° ratings are typically collected so the raters remain anonymous; if not anonymous, raters will more likely inflate the ratings. Anonymous ratings have potential drawbacks if used for evaluation purposes. For example, if a company used anonymous 360° ratings as part of the documentation for a personnel action involving a manager, such as a demotion, dismissal, or unattained promotion or pay raise, that manager could potentially make a legal case against the firm. Specifically, because the ratings are anonymous, no one can trace them to specific individuals, and hence the ratings' validity could come into question in a court action.

Using 360° ratings for evaluation also becomes a problem if only a minority of a manager's raters complete surveys or if the manager has so few raters in a rating category, for example direct reports, that anonymity cannot be assured. What proportion of the surveys need to be returned to ensure a representative sample of ratings? What can be done with managers who have few direct reports, no real customers, or few peers? Will some managers therefore be evaluated with 360° input while others are not? Such issues could present equity or perhaps even legal problems if a firm bases promotions on different types of information for different managers.

A company should only use ratings for evaluative purposes when the raters have fully committed to the goals of the organization, rather than merely their own personal goals. Oftentimes, this is not the case, and raters' primary concerns involve their own short-term needs. For example, a subordinate may only provide high upward feedback ratings to a manager who maintains the status quo, that is, a manager who does not provide a high degree of challenge to that individual's job. On the other hand, that individual and the organization may need exactly that.

This suggests another caution regarding ratings: Be careful what you measure! If a manager's ratings depend on creating a positive or relaxed climate, this factor may actually take away from work directly geared toward bottom-line results. For example, customers may call the manager away from the office frequently or necessitate many hours on the phone, thus making the manager less available to employees. If the manager's customer-oriented behavior is not part of the criteria measured, it will diminish over time, and the manager will replace it with more frequent interaction with employees. Yes, relationships with employees may improve, but at what cost?

Certainly, not all experts agree that using 360° feedback for evaluation necessarily creates problems. If traditional appraisal depends on the opinion of one person, the supervisor, who is not always in the best position to judge and is never anonymous, would 360° appraisal not be an improvement, even if not always totally honest? When more sources offer input, the ratee likely will feel the rating is more fair and will feel more satisfied with the appraisal process. However, given the companies that have abandoned the use of 360° appraisal, one should question just what leads to positive and negative attitudes toward the process.

If companies take the above posture—that 360° feedback, while not perfect, still offers an improvement over traditional appraisal—, as mentioned earlier the authors would caution them to take it slowly. Use 360° feedback strictly for development first. Let managers and others become comfortable with the process and let them have time to make necessary changes in their behaviors. Once employees see the unlikelihood of negative repercussions and that the information truly does help, they will have less apprehension about using 360° ratings for evaluation.

A CASE IN POINT: STUDENT EVALUATIONS OF TEACHING

A pertinent example of using customer/upward feedback for those in academia involves student evaluations of teaching effectiveness. Beginning mainly in the 1970s, student evaluations have provided a form of customer-based feedback—some might argue upward feedback—to faculty members at colleges and universities. In line with institutional theory, such evaluations have become so commonplace in colleges and universities as to represent an institutional norm. That is, any university that might consider dropping student evaluations would probably be branded as unconcerned about teaching. In their early years, student evaluations were designed mainly as developmental tools, providing faculty with information useful for improving teaching. Over time, university administrators have increasingly used this feedback for evaluative purposes, such as for promotion and tenure decisions.

One might wonder whether this feedback process has resulted in improved student-faculty relationships, trust, communication, and so forth. Has this process had any effect, either positive or negative, on the bottom line, which includes student learning outcomes and the satisfaction of the ultimate customers, that is, employers and society? The clear possibility exists that student feedback, especially when used for evaluation as opposed to development, can modify a teacher's style but has no, or even a negative, impact on student learning. For example, will students rate instructors highly if they demand a lot and grade hard? Or are students more likely to value an easy going style and sense of humor, both of which may not always facilitate student learning.

A recent example experienced by one of the authors illustrates this point. In a write-in comment, a student who provided low ratings indicated that s/he would prefer that the instructor not have such high standards of grammar and writing style with regard to required course papers. If a university allows such comments and associated ratings to form the basis of an instructor's evaluation, chances increase that instructors will indeed lower their standards. This could serve the short-term needs of the customer, or student, by making it easier to obtain higher grades and positive feedback. However, in the long run, lowering standards would shortchange customer needs when the student is perceived as a poor writer in future contexts. Moreover, the needs of other customer groups, such as future employers and society as a whole, would not be met if colleges and universities routinely allow students who have not been held to rigorous standards to graduate. In short, the underlying problem is that, similar to numerous organizations, those in academia have lacked clear goals and a clear understanding of the complexity of the various internal and external customer groups. Nor have they had good outcome measures for their student feedback process—a process now used exclusively to evaluate teaching effectiveness at virtually all colleges and universities throughout the country.

WHERE ARE THE DATA?

A problem related to the absence of clear purpose involves the absence of clear data. As noted in the previous chapter, in recent telephone interviews conducted with individuals who spearheaded the implementation of

360° feedback in a number of *Fortune* 500 companies, the availability of effectiveness data was discouraging. Specifically, the only data available about the outcome(s) of 360° feedback involved employee and manager perceptions of the process, random anecdotes, and on rare occasions, changes in employee ratings of managers before and after feedback. Recent research in a retail store setting showed that subordinate and peer ratings increased from Time 1 to Time 2 after receiving 360° feedback at Time 1, but managers' ratings from their supervisors and customers did not change. In addition, this research revealed that the 360° feedback intervention did not affect store sales volume.[7]

Some data suggest productivity improvements among college and university faculty and improved customer satisfaction ratings after the implementation of 360° feedback. However, the research generating these data did not include control groups, so it is difficult to conclude that 360° processes solely caused the improvements.[8]

With so little evidence of bottom-line impact or even organizational culture change, a logical question becomes: Why do companies spend so much money and devote so many employee work-hours to 360° feedback processes? As argued above, part of the craze may simply be because of the previously mentioned institutional effects or keeping up with the Joneses. Perhaps organizations engage in these activities because it is humanistically appropriate to increase managers' self-awareness. Alternatively, many organizational cultures have progressed to the point where any program designed to increase feedback seems like the right thing to do.

However, few organizations today can afford to engage in costly training or development activities purely altruistically or on the basis of speculative success. Rather, many decision makers and participants need convincing that they can expect the development effort to impact the bottom line in some way, at some time. Indeed, if managers are not convinced, they may attempt to stonewall implementation efforts, perhaps simply by not participating or by discouraging the 360° raters, such as subordinates, from participating. The result could include low response rates to surveys, lack of follow-up with subordinates in the case of upward feedback or with peers and customers in the case of broader 360° feedback, little motivation to change, or increased employee expectations with no results.

The remainder of this chapter will focus on the need to critically evaluate 360° feedback implementation efforts. In doing so, the chapter will outline specific recommendations for organizations before and during implementation.

EVALUATING 360° FEEDBACK EFFORTS

The above arguments suggest that, regarding the effects of 360° feedback programs in organizations, much more is *not* known than is actually known. This phenomenon can be likened to the mushroom theory of management: "Keep them in the dark, feed them a lot of &¢$#%, and hope they'll grow." Unfortunately, the mushroom theory has not received much empirical support.

Perhaps a number of obstacles exist that prevent the collection or dissemination of real data and results. Some of these are quite intuitive and include managerial desires for action, as opposed to stringent evaluation. Some managers may simply think, "We know it works, so let's get on with it. Why else would so many organizations use it?" The desire for action leads to a mentality that stresses activity-centered programs, as opposed to results-driven programs.[9] That is, things such as response rates and the number of managers receiving feedback reports are stressed instead of things like improved managerial performance and higher customer satisfaction. This does not suggest that activity-based measurement has no importance. Rather, expected results, including those of both short- and long-term natures, must also be articulated and measured.

Fuzzier obstacles may include consultants' or internal champions' fears of not having concrete results to show after investing time and money into 360° feedback programs. For example, senior management in one mid-sized insurance company was very reluctant to allow a colleague of the authors to conduct research to determine if a strong relationship existed between individual work performance and what the company's 360° appraisal process measured. Management feared that if the research results showed no relationship between performance and behavior existed, it might have to stop using 360° appraisals. Perhaps even more relevant, consultants/internal champions may not clearly understand what outcomes to measure or when to measure them.

Recommendation 1: *Make consultants/internal champions accountable for results.*

This recommendation may seem obvious, but how often are the people who push 360° feedback systems told they must go into the process with specific goals, realistic timetables, and a plan for measuring results? This event rarely occurs. Instead, consultants may jump on the 360° bandwagon, put together enticing packages, and subsequently feel reluctant to charge companies for evaluation. They may also fear responses such as "Why do you need to evaluate this? I thought you said it worked." Or perhaps an internal management development or human resource specialist wants to impress executives by championing 360° feedback processes. This all results in a rush to implementation without a clear understanding of needs or expected results.

Of course, a conflict of interest can result when program evaluation is left in the hands of people who have either marketed or championed a process. Organizations must take care that they have objective evaluation processes with verifiable data.

Recommendation 2: Engage in a pilot test initiative.

As mentioned previously, managers tend to favor immediate action, and conversely, a pilot study or test implies restrained action. A reasonable pilot study could last a year or longer. However, the benefits of a pilot study can be immense. Obviously, the ability to recognize possible problems before they spin out of control provides an advantage. It is also important to assess the readiness of the organization's climate and culture for such an intervention. In organizations with traditional hierarchies, this inversion of the organizational pyramid can be threatening and problematic.

Most of the consultants with whom the authors have talked have reinforced the need for pilot studies but also added that few companies conduct them. The authors did run a pilot test in a few departments before full-scale implementation in the large telecommunication company mentioned previously, and the results strongly reinforced the advantages of pilot testing. They identified modifiable problems with the original survey items. They discovered both employee and managerial resistance and fear, which they counteracted with general information sessions for all employees in the targeted departments. They identified concerns with confidentiality and anonymity that stemmed from an earlier survey intervention by another company in which breaches of confidentiality were suspected. As such, the authors presented their strategies for ensuring anonymity and confidentiality to ease these concerns. Because these problems were corrected, the authors implemented a relatively smooth rollout across the division and realized high survey response rates. In addition, they followed up the pilot group before implementation and obtained initial effectiveness data. Their ability to demonstrate success on a small scale helped convince reluctant managers that the rollout would benefit the company.

Recommendation 3: Create focus group(s) to identify effectiveness criteria measures.

The list of possible effectiveness criteria measures for a 360° feedback program can be quite extensive. Measures should focus on activity levels as well as results. Possibilities include:

1. Ratee and rater reactions to the program, in other words, the extent to which they believe the process has value;
2. Response rates—obviously a program cannot succeed if potential raters do not respond when surveyed;
3. Grievance rates;
4. Customer satisfaction;
5. Employee satisfaction;
6. Absenteeism/turnover;
7. Work behaviors, for example leadership, communication, and employee development efforts; and
8. Work performance, such as individual work output or contributions to work unit output.

The best way to ensure criteria will be ultimately scrutinized is, with the help of the consultants, to form one or more focus groups early on. The groups could be composed of a combination of line managers, management development specialists, human resource specialists, and others. These groups should respond to the question, "What do you think would improve around here if those being rated got better at the dimensions on which they receive ratings?" The groups should be pressed for specifics and then guided to systematically monitor progress on the identified criteria before 360° feedback begins and after it has been fully implemented.

One possibility that should not be overlooked is the use of carefully collected anecdotes. Anecdotes are often collected unsystematically, thus reflecting hearsay. In contrast, anecdotes of both successes and failures could potentially be collected in a more systematic fashion, for example with open-ended survey or interview questions. These anecdotes could then be considered openly and weighed and balanced to indicate the relative success of a 360° feedback program.

Recommendation 4: *Evaluate using a pre/post–control group design.*

Evaluation of the process helps accomplish the organization's goals and ensures that it works as intended. Optimally, at least in the early stages, the organization should adopt a pre/post–control group design to assess the impact of the process. That is, the company should measure behaviors and outcomes prior to feedback, as well as after feedback and should select some individuals to take part while not selecting others.

Ideally, the organization would create three groups, selecting participants randomly, to begin the evaluation phase. Exhibit 4-1 displays the process. Group 1 would complete surveys, and outcome measures would be assessed at Time 1. At Time 2, Group 1 would receive feedback. At Time 3, at least six months later, surveys would be readministered and outcomes would be reassessed. Group 2 would complete surveys and assess outcomes at Times 1 and 3 but receive no feedback, thus sensitizing this group to the behaviors of interest as measured by the surveys but with no individual feedback to managers. In this way, the impact of surveying alone can be assessed relative to the impact of surveying and feedback. Group 3 would receive no surveys or feedback and would only complete surveys and outcome assessments at Time 3. In this way, the organization can assess the impact of feedback, as well as the impact of merely surveying employees.

Exhibit 4-1
Possible Evaluation Study Design

	Time 1	Time 2	Time 3	Time 4
	360° Survey & Outcome Assessment	Feedback	360° Survey & Outcome Assessment	Feedback
Group 1	X	X	X	X
Group 2	X		X	X
Group 3 (control group)			X	X

This recommendation may cut against the grain of typical managerial thinking for two reasons. First, many managers assume that if something is worth doing, it is worth doing for everybody right now. Second, many managers do not like the idea of someone using their people as guinea pigs. Managers should reconsider this line of thought. In fact, a company could implement the evaluation design in Exhibit 4-1 simply by beginning the process in stages in various parts of the organization. As also shown in Exhibit 4-1, the process might go like this:

1. Survey Groups 1 and 2;

2. Give feedback to Group 1;

3. Resurvey Groups 1 and 2;

4. Survey Group 3 for the first time; and

5. Give feedback to all groups at Time 4 after collecting post-feedback evaluative data for Groups 1 and 2.

In this way, a company can make comparisons between groups not surveyed, those surveyed but that have not received feedback, and those that have received feedback. A sample question that could be answered based on this design is: Is feedback really important, or is the simple act of surveying sufficient to stimulate behavior change? Chances are good that portions of the organization, such as Group 3 above, have survived and can continue to survive without 360° feedback, at least for some time. Moreover, if throughout the program evaluation process the company uses the feedback strictly for developmental purposes, no one should protest about unfair or inconsistent treatment. At the same time, if over time the program shifts toward more evaluative purposes such as using 360° ratings for pay or promotion purposes, a company should enact additional program evaluation.

Clearly, more experimental field studies on 360° feedback are needed. Therefore, academic institutions and business organizations should establish research partnerships with each other. Another area that obviously needs research involves the question of whether improvements in managerial or leadership behaviors based on 360° feedback in turn *cause* improvements in work unit or department performance. Also, do the improvements have an effect on employee satisfaction, intention to leave the work unit or the organization, absenteeism, or turnover? With proper control of other factors that could affect results, it is possible to determine what to do to improve the 360° feedback process and ultimately whether the process is worth the time, money and effort.

Recommendation 5: Be careful what is measured and how it's used.

As mentioned above, ratings can and often do drive behavior. Even when a company uses ratings strictly for developmental purposes, individuals tend to modify behaviors to receive more positive ratings. Therefore, for 360° surveys to reflect those behaviors that the organization ranks high in importance, companies should also take care to ensure that the measured behaviors closely relate to the accomplishment of the organization's goals.

Referring again to the example of student evaluations of teaching, on the positive side this example of upward feedback should encourage better teaching styles and classroom relationships. Communication between instructors and students should also improve. Problems along these lines have evidenced themselves in college and university settings in the past. The implementation of student feedback processes has fostered improvements in these areas.

However, such a process may also encourage behaviors and outcomes that do not benefit customers. Instructors may avoid trying to challenge students for fear of upsetting them and obtaining lower student evaluations at the end of the semester. Specifically, instructors may make assignments and readings easier, and faculty may hesitate to disagree with students' comments or concerns for fear of appearing disagreeable. Moreover, sensing that students dislike ambiguity, instructors may "teach the test," meaning they may virtually announce their exams' contents through the use of study guides, and provide a lockstep method of accomplishing assignments and research projects. The growing phenomenon of grade inflation should not surprise anyone. Of course, the problem remains that academia's ultimate customers, society and future employers, need and seek students who have encountered challenges and can adequately deal with ambiguity in solving problems—this is what the real world is all about. Future employers and graduate schools want to look at a grade point average that has meaning as a selection criterion, and this increasingly is not the case. In short, although this example of upward feedback can provide valuable information for its academic recipients, people generally modify their behavior to fit what gets measured and rewarded. Such behavior may not always work toward long-term goals and outcomes.

Recommendation 6: Train raters.

Almost all 360° instruments rely on rating scales. Research has clearly established that raters commit different types of rating errors, such as rating too leniently or too harshly.[10] Some raters play it safe by consistently using the central rating points. Other errors include halo effects, or generalizing high ratings on one dimension to other potentially unobserved dimensions, and recency effects, or weighting information received most recently most heavily. Therefore, rater training is absolutely essential to increase the possibility that individuals will obtain valid ratings from others. Raters need training in how to complete rating forms and how to avoid making possible rating errors. Rater training should also cover the objectives of the surveys and the overall process. Such training may be especially critical for new 360° feedback initiatives because the chosen raters may have little experience performing the rating process, as is often the case for subordinates of first-level supervisors.

As an example, UPS does rater training by sensitizing raters to potential rating errors, explaining the appraisal feedback process, and discussing how the firm will use the data. In addition, a few medium-sized organizations in the Midwest indicated to a colleague of the authors that they provide raters with frame-of-reference training. Such training includes covering the roles, responsibilities, and accountabilities of the ratee. The training links survey items to roles and responsibilities to help the various raters create common frames of reference when they evaluate ratees. To improve observations, raters receive surveys to keep throughout the year where they can record observations of incidents that would help them determine final ratings. UPS encourages raters to use their records of work incidents and to supplement their ratings with written feedback. The company asks raters to comment on what they would like a ratee to do more of, do less of, and continue to do. Raters know that providing written feedback is entirely voluntary. Some raters express concern about losing the anonymity of their responses. However, according to the HRM directors in these organizations, raters thus far take risks to provide ratees with specific written comments. Furthermore, the amount of written feedback has remained about the same during the last three years. Finally, ratees indicated the written feedback is more valuable to them than numerical ratings.

OPENING CASE REVISITED

What did the organization described at the beginning of this chapter do about the 360° feedback program it started? Management decided to start over and took the next year to engage in several important activities. The first involved developing a 360° feedback project team composed of representative employees from different areas and levels of the organization. The team sought to design, implement, and evaluate a 360° feedback process acceptable to organizational members that would produce results. The team defined the following outcomes:

1. Improve communication by reducing the undiscussables between raters and ratees;

2. Increase alignment of expectations between raters and ratees; and

3. Improve ratees' work behaviors and performance.

The team, facilitated by the consultants, conceptualized how the 360° process should work to produce results. The team decided to develop its own 360° feedback survey items based on values the organization deemed important and also decided to include a written feedback section on the survey. With the help of consultants, pilot tests of survey items were conducted before producing the survey for use in a rollout. In addition, the team put the survey online using the computer network. This online process maintained anonymity and eliminated the need for someone outside the organization to type the written comments. Raters, ratees, and coaches, who are those selected to help feedback recipients formulate and implement action plans, received training about different aspects of the 360° process.

The project team decided to administer 360° surveys throughout the year. This procedure addressed the issue of overburdening people with filling out surveys within one particular month, as done previously. The team wanted the 360° process to provide individuals with valuable information they could use to set specific improvement goals and action plans. The company expected individuals to review their 360° results with their respective coaches, who then helped prepare them for a discussion of appropriate 360° results with their respective raters. Thus, the company expected managers to share the results of their upward appraisals with people reporting directly to them and to share the results of their peer feedback with their peers. These events took place during regularly scheduled meetings. The HRM area helped by providing facilitation, if needed, when managers shared results with their raters. In sum, the 360° feedback process became a way of life in the organization with heavy emphasis on improving communication regarding expectations of workplace behaviors, and accountability to improve behaviors based on 360° feedback.

Based on input from focus groups, the team also decided that the purpose of the 360° feedback process was primarily developmental but with accountability. That is, individuals needed to use the feedback to set developmental goals. Although this company did not specifically use 360° feedback in appraisal, feedback becomes implicitly evaluative when a company asks raters to share *data* with supervisors. As part of this company's process, individuals had to meet with their supervisors and share the data. Supervisors subsequently held them responsible for attaining their developmental goals. Consequences for failing to meet developmental goals ranged from being put on notice, or the corrective action track, after the second round of 360° feedback if no improvements occurred in the work behaviors targeted for improvement, to potential demotion if no changes occurred after three years. Furthermore, the company would use 360° feedback information in annual performance appraisals only in cases of obvious need for corrective action and/or demotion.

Furthermore, in conjunction with the consultant, the company designed a three-year research program to assess the 360° process. Research questions were formulated, and a research proposal was submitted to senior management. For example, one research question asked whether the individuals trained to seek additional, follow-up feedback from respondents actually obtain more feedback and positive outcomes than those who did not receive such training. Several meetings took place with management to explain the rationale for the research questions and the reasons for experimental field studies. In some instances it was not possible to get complete randomization. Therefore, a quasi-experimental design was substituted to examine the effects of the process. That study is currently ongoing.

Finally, the company formed a 360° feedback steering committee, consisting of one member of the board of directors, one manager each at senior, middle, and first-line levels, and three employees. The committee is similar in nature to the steering committees that provide structure and guidance to total quality management initiatives. During the next three years, the committee holds original project team and consultants accountable. Issues to consider include long-term strategic uses of 360° feedback, whether ratees and their groups achieve positive outcomes, and short-term problems, such as cases of perceived retribution against respondents.

CONCLUSIONS

In many organizations, people may view 360° feedback as just another management fad or flavor of the month. Employees and managers have seen a number of change initiatives begin with much hoopla and fanfare, only to end abruptly and often with little apparent reason. Managerial actions and initiatives that occur in the present can never totally separate from those in the past—at least not in the minds of organizational members who stand to be affected. In other words, people tend to remember, or they will tell new employees stories about, actions or initiatives that have occurred in the past. Over time, people grow weary of such initiatives and even become cynical with regard to their possible success. These people may view new initiatives, such as 360° feedback, as knee-jerk reactions to some problem such as increased competition and lack of internal communication, and thus they may think they should just wait until the storm blows over.

Obviously, organizations, like individuals, cannot erase their pasts. However, at the same time, it is possible to keep new initiatives like 360° feedback from running amok and, conversely, to realize degrees of success. The opening case in this chapter provides lessons to avoid faddism and the potential cynicism it engenders. Specifically, this case demonstrates the need to systematically determine how a company will use 360° feedback and what outcomes the company can expect. The case also shows how the process should be tailored to the needs of the organization and subsequently scrutinized in terms of careful evaluation. In general, all aspects of the process must be held accountable, and this is why the organization formed a steering committee for the long term. With careful planning and implementation, companies can realize the benefits of 360° feedback.

The next chapter focuses more specifically on how 360° feedback can impact individual behavior and performance. Later chapters will expand the discussion beyond the individual level and will consider how 360° feedback can connect to organizational culture and performance.

REFERENCES

1. The authors are indebted to David Antonioni for supplying much of the information relevant to this case.

2. For a more complete description of resource dependence theory, see:
   D. Ulrich and J. Barney, "Perspectives in Organizations: Resource Dependence, Efficiency, and Population," *Academy of Management Review,* 9 (1984), pp. 471–481.
   C. Oliver, "Strategic Responses to Institutional Processes," *Academy of Management Review,* 16 (1991), pp. 145–179.

3. For a more complete description of institutional theory, see P. S. Tolbert, "Institutional Environments and Resource Dependence: Sources of Administrative Structure in Institutions for Higher Education," *Administrative Science Quarterly,* 30 (1985), pp. 1–13.

4. The importance of rewarding desired behavior was clearly elaborated by Steven Kerr in a 1975 classic article that has recently been republished and expanded: S. Kerr, "On the Folly of Rewarding A, While Hoping for B," *Academy of Management Executive,* 9(1) (1995), pp. 7–16.

5. See:
   H. Bernardin, S. Dahmus, and G. Redmon, "Attitudes of First-Line Supervisors Toward Subordinate Appraisals," Human Resource Management, 32 (1993), pp. 315–324.
   A. Michels, "More Employees Evaluate the Boss," Fortune (July 29, 1991), p. 13.

6. C. Timmreck and D. Bracken, "Multisource Assessment: Reinforcing the Preferred 'Means' to the End," (paper presented at the meeting of the Society for Industrial and Organizational Psychology, San Diego, 1996).

7. See J. Bernardin, C. Hagan, and J. Kane, "The Effects of a 360-Degree Appraisal System on Managerial Performance: No Matter How Cynical I Get, I Can't Keep Up," *Upward Feedback: The Ups and Downs of It* (symposium conducted at the tenth annual conference of the Society for Industrial and Organizational Psychology, Orlando, 1995).

8. See Mark Edwards' and Ann Ewen's accounts of productivity improvement and improved customer satisfaction ratings following a 360° feedback intervention in their book, *360-Degree Feedback* (New York: AMACOM, 1996).

9. The issue of activity-centered programs versus results-driven programs is discussed in more depth in the following article: R. H. Shaffer and H. A. Thompson, "Successful Change Programs Begin With Results," *Harvard Business Review,* 70 (January/February 1992), pp. 80–89.

10. See F. J. Landy and J. L. Farr, "Performance Rating," *Psychological Bulletin,* 87 (1980), pp. 82–107.

CHAPTER 5

How Does 360° Feedback Impact Individual Performance?

THE RELEVANCE OF SELF-AWARENESS

"To be effective and indeed to simply survive in organizations, managers must understand the ineffective actions they take so that they can correct them. They need to develop an accurate view of how they are being perceived."[1]

For years psychologists and management researchers such as Susan Ashford made the case that seeing oneself as others do is important to an individual's psychological health and, in turn, his or her ability to work successfully with others in organizations. In today's work environment, the number of constituents to whom individuals must respond is increasing, making this accurate view of oneself more difficult to acquire. It is no longer sufficient to acquire feedback only from one's supervisor to get a fairly accurate view of oneself as seen by others.

Accountability to customers, both internal and external, has been a hot topic in the 1990s and will sustain its importance in the next decade. The proliferation of teams—work teams, project teams, problem-solving teams, and so forth—requires increased attention to peer relationships. And clearly, workers demand more from supervisors in terms of becoming involved in determining work processes and in problem solving, which increases the needs for interaction and accountability among the leaders and the led. Consequently, it is now up to managers, as well as employees, to understand how many constituencies perceive them as they become self-aware and, optimally, responsive to others.

360° FEEDBACK TO THE RESCUE

Three hundred sixty–degree feedback has helped answer the call for increased self-awareness and improved individual performance. A manager or employee can now receive anonymous feedback from peers, customers, and subordinates in addition to feedback from supervisors and compare that feedback to his or her self-assessment. The comparisons of self-ratings and other ratings highlight blindspots, or areas where the target receives lower ratings by others than by self; and averaged scores from each rater group highlight overall strengths and weaknesses. Exhibit 5-1 depicts the 360° feedback process and the means by which it impacts individual outcomes.

The process begins with knowledgeable observers, as well as the target individual, completing surveys about the individual's job-relevant behavior. Peers, subordinates, and customers complete surveys anonymously. Supervisors, because there is usually only one, also complete surveys, but without anonymity. The feedback is then aggregated by rater group and provided in report form to the target individual. The individual is then encouraged to seek additional feedback from raters to clarify and expand upon the written feedback provided in the report. If the report identifies blindspots or weaknesses, and if the target accepts the feedback as valid and useful, greater self-awareness should result. Additionally, the discrepancies between self-perception and others' perceptions will lead the target to implicitly or explicitly set improvement goals. Both the increased self-awareness and the improvement goals will lead to improved performance and attitudes, providing the organizational systems and supports, such as reward systems and training, exist to support such change. Each of the elements and processes highlighted in the Exhibit 5-1 model will be described in more detail later in this chapter.

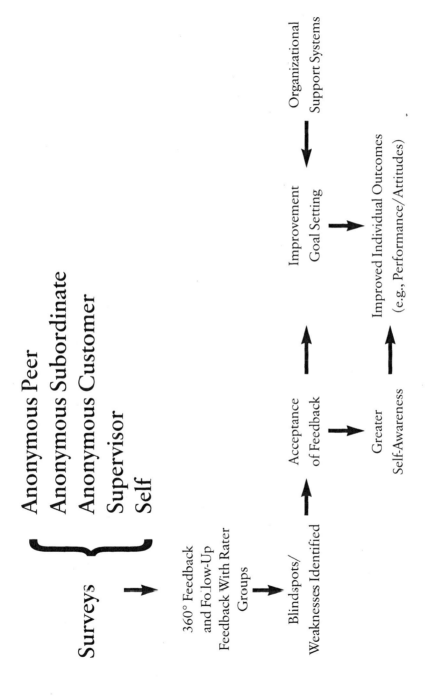

Exhibit 5-1. The Means by Which 360° Feedback Impacts Individual Outcomes

The rationale behind the feedback process is that when individuals become aware of blindspots or weaknesses, they will be motivated to improve. And because the information comes from a variety of sources, it will be richer and will provide more—and perhaps more accurate and thus more readily accepted—feedback than the individual could receive from only a supervisor.

Why might the information from a variety of sources have more use than that from a supervisor? One reason is that the nature of jobs is changing. No longer is the supervisor the only individual with relevant information about an employee's job performance. Indeed, in some cases, supervisors may have few opportunities to observe a subordinate's job performance. For many people, their employees, customers, peers, team members, and/or subordinates have better opportunities to assess behaviors relevant to effective job performance. Plus, more sources of feedback means more vantage points.

More sources of feedback, particularly when the feedback provided by subordinates, peers, or customers is averaged, also means any particular individual's biases carry less weight, and thus, more accurate assessments should result. And perhaps most importantly, supervisor feedback by its very nature is not anonymous. Supervisors often avoid providing negative, or even positive, feedback because they find the face-to-face feedback process uncomfortable. They may fear retribution, defensiveness, or decreased morale from the recipients if they provide negative feedback, and judging from the reactions individuals have had to negative performance appraisals, they would not be entirely without cause.[2] Because feedback from groups of peers, subordinates, or customers can be anonymous, it is likely to be more honest and accurate. The fact that it comes from a number of individuals makes it more difficult to discount, and retribution is unlikely as the specific person or persons providing the negative feedback are unknown. In one study, the authors asked the individuals who had provided feedback, subordinates in this case, if they had experienced any negative repercussions from supervisors after their supervisors received the feedback. Less than 2 percent felt a supervisor had reacted negatively in anyway. So 360° feedback should provide valuable information to the individual manager or employee from a variety of sources.

However, the validity of the feedback only provides part of the equation if feedback is to motivate positive change. Certainly, the feedback recipient needs to see the feedback as valid and useful if he or she is to use it. But other factors also affect how the recipient will receive and use the feedback. One factor that impacts the usefulness of the feedback is whether it confirms or disconfirms the recipient's self-assessment.

Types of Feedback

Basically, an individual could receive four types of feedback from a feedback source:

1. *Confirmatory positive feedback:* The individual receives high ratings from others, which confirm the individual's high self-ratings.

2. *Disconfirmatory negative feedback:* The individual receives ratings from others that are lower than his or her self-assessment.

3. *Confirmatory negative feedback:* The ratings received from others are low, and the self-ratings also are low.

4. *Disconfirmatory positive feedback:* The individual's self-ratings are lower than ratings received by others.

What constitutes higher or lower depends on the rating scale used, as well as the variance among ratees. Generally, on a five-point scale, half a standard deviation difference indicates a score that is notably higher or lower than the self-rating.

Depending on the type of feedback received, the degree of acceptance among individuals receiving feedback can be predicted. First, individuals will most readily accept positive information consistent with their self-perceptions, or confirmatory positive feedback. The feedback merely confirms the good job the recipient thinks he or she does. In this case the feedback can be positively reinforcing and help maintain desirable behaviors.

However, the most common type of feedback is not confirmatory positive feedback but disconfirmatory negative feedback. Disconfirmatory negative feedback, while unpleasant to receive, is the most likely to motivate changes in behavior if accepted as valid. If the recipient acknowledges some truth in the negative feedback, it motivates changes in behavior because it arouses dissonance between the recipient's self-perception and the feedback received, and the inconsistency causes discomfort to the recipient. This state of discomfort often motivates the individual to make corrections in behavior to minimize the self-other discrepancy. However, negative feedback does not always motivate positive behavior change. Individuals sometimes react to negative feedback with defensiveness, denial, or other attempts to discount its validity. Negative feedback also can demotivate if the individual does not feel he or she can change in the desired direction. Later, this chapter will discuss the relevance of follow-up and training as they pertain to negative feedback and the belief that one can change, as well as techniques for increasing acceptance.

A third type of feedback, confirmatory negative feedback, involves negative feedback that confirms a negative self-perception. Generally, research has shown that this individual will not likely change.[3] Perhaps this person suffers from burnout or is demotivated for some other reason, but when the negative ratings from others confirm negative self-ratings, feedback offers little motivational value in prompting behavior change in response to the feedback.

The fourth type of feedback is disconfirmatory positive feedback. These individuals receive feedback that is more positive than their self-ratings. Generally this type of feedback provides positive reinforcement or a sense of reward and perpetuates a continuation of desired behavior. It may, however, lead the recipient of the positive feedback to rate himself or herself higher in the future, indicating that perhaps the individual's self-perception has become more positive as a result of feedback.[4]

Also, individuals receiving 360° feedback often receive different types of feedback from different sources. For example, supervisors may rate an individual high on cooperation, yet peers rate the individual low on cooperation. Feedback recipients tend to view feedback from the group that most impacts their outcomes, such as pay, raises, and promotions, as most important. This is generally, though not always, the supervisor. Feedback recipients also tend to discount negative feedback from one group if they get positive feedback from another. In a recent 360° feedback session conducted by the authors, the reactions from participants confirmed this response. Participants seemed to believe they were doing all right if their supervisors rated them above average, regardless of how subordinates or peers rated them. The authors pointed out that their supervisors were not providing anonymous feedback so it may have been biased in a positive direction and also emphasized that their success as supervisors depended a great deal on how well they supervised their subordinates and interacted with peers. In other words, supervisors were not the only sources with relevant feedback.

Consequently, it is important to encourage feedback recipients to attend to feedback from *all* sources, as each source reflects some unique aspects of individuals' effectiveness. The importance of perceptions should be stressed. If a subordinate does not believe her manager listens well, the subordinate's perception, not reality, impacts the supervisor/subordinate relationship. Feedback recipients also should be encouraged to understand why different rating sources may perceive different levels of skill in different areas and what they can do to obtain a more uniform perception.

Why Are Self-Other Rating Discrepancies So Common?

Research has shown that self-perceptions and self-ratings tend to agree with others' ratings and objective criterion measures less than do ratings provided by others.[5] And most often, the self-ratings are inflated. This suggests self-ratings often have less accuracy than those provided by others. This does not mean other ratings are always accurate. Other perceptions and ratings also may be inaccurate. The following list summarizes several factors that contribute to differing perceptions and ratings.

Factors That Contribute to Self-Other Discrepancies in Perceptions and Ratings

☐ Ego preservation for the self-rater

☐ Reluctance to give negative feedback

☐ Differing information

☐ Purposeful rating distortions

☐ Stereotypes and biases

☐ Emotions, such as fear

☐ Attitudes, such as liking

☐ Cognitive processing, such as selective attention

First, individuals generally prefer to see themselves in a positive light. This may mean they ignore, distort, rationalize, or give less importance to negative information than positive information in an attempt to preserve their egos. Second, the reluctance of individuals to give face-to-face negative feedback contributes to individuals' tendencies to hold overly positive self-perceptions. In other words, to some extent the negative feedback most people deserve has been withheld or distorted. Because people withhold or sugarcoat negative feedback, individuals believe they perform better than they actually do. Incidentally, the tendency to withhold or sugarcoat diminishes when people can anonymously give feedback. Third, self-raters often do not have the same amount of comparative information about how others are doing as do other observers, such as supervisors. Those who have more comparative information tend to make more accurate judgments and provide more accurate ratings. For example, supervisors generally have more information about the performance of their many subordinates than any single subordinate has about another. Supervisors are responsible for performance and performance appraisals and thus will more likely be astute to interindividual differences. Fourth, individuals, particularly self-raters, tend to distort ratings if they believe the ratings they provide will impact the outcomes received, such as raises and promotions.[6] In the case of self-ratings, individuals distort toward the positive end of the scale.

Observer ratings may succumb to several types of distortions. First, people can distort ratings downward if they intend retribution. In one particular case, a subordinate indicated she would never give her supervisor anything but the lowest ratings because she felt he had discriminated against her in a promotion decision three years earlier. Second, stereotypes or biases may influence observers, particularly when they have limited information. For example, if one holds a stereotype that engineers tend to have poor interpersonal skills, and if an internal customer, for example someone in production, rating an engineer has had few interactions with the engineer, that rater may rate the engineer low on interpersonal skills because it is consistent with his or her stereotype of engineers. Alternatively, biases such as the halo effect can contribute to distortions in that a rater may rate another individual high in unobserved dimensions if the individual's performance has been high in one area. Emotions and attitudes, such as fear, jealousy, liking, disliking, and so forth, on the part of raters can affect ratings and cause them to be less accurate and dissimilar to self-ratings. Third, when supervisors rate subordinates they may tend to inflate the ratings because they feel responsible for their subordinates' performance or because they believe having good subordinates enhances their image. This type of influence most often appears when ratings are not anonymous or when they will be used to influence outcomes for the ratee.

Information differences also impact the agreement between self-other perceptions and ratings. Different individuals receive different information. For example, an individual's self-rating of listening skills may be based on how he or she performs in a variety of contexts, whereas the same person's subordinates may only have observed the ratee in one or two contexts. In other words, the information the self-rater and his or her subordinates have could certainly differ.

Cognitive processing variables affect ratings as well. These include selective attention, or remembering the most important things; primacy, or remembering information received first; and recency, or remembering information received most recently.

The myriad of factors discussed above suggests that many things can affect the accuracy and honesty of ratings, thereby contributing to self-other differences and, for that matter, other-other differences as well. Multisource feedback diminishes the impact of individual biases and influences because an average includes many scores; therefore it is a useful addition to feedback from only one non-anonymous source, such as the supervisor. This does not mean companies should eliminate supervisor ratings. Clearly, most feedback recipients have great interest in ratings from their supervisors, and these ratings also provide useful points of comparison with other rating sources.[7] However, given the potential for bias or distortion, supervisor ratings may not be the most valid.

To further improve the validity of feedback responses, some experts advocate trimming scores, which means dropping the extreme, or the highest and lowest, scores when computing the averages. This is similar to the way the Olympics incorporates judges' ratings into an athlete's score. This practice can help remove a particular response tendency or bias but only works well when the feedback recipient has a sizeable number of raters.

How Can Individuals Be Expected to React to Feedback?

Because disconfirming negative feedback is most likely to promote changes in behavior, it will be considered first. In a way, similar to a negative performance appraisal, disconfirming negative feedback can be likened to punishment. When people are told they are not doing as well as they thought, it feels like punishment. The studies of punishment suggest the following possibilities in response to punishment.

Possible Reactions to Disconfirming Negative Feedback

☐ Motivation to change in a positive direction

☐ Defensiveness—"They rated me poorly because I make them work hard."

☐ Denial—"This must be someone else's data!"

☐ Disbelief—"The computer made a mistake."

☐ Anger—"Those dirty rats!"

☐ Disappointment—"How could they feel that way?"

☐ Poor job attitudes

☐ Less commitment to the organization

☐ Less commitment to raters who provided negative feedback

One possibility is that the negative feedback will motivate the ratee. As mentioned earlier, some individuals will find the inconsistency between their self-perceptions and the feedback they receive uncomfortable, and they will make behavior changes in hopes of receiving more positive ratings/evaluations in the future. These more positive ratings more closely conform to the individual's self-perception, and thus, the inconsistency is reduced. This desired outcome of negative feedback would most likely result if the ratee perceives the feedback as genuine and constructive.

However, other potential effects of punishment, or negative performance appraisals, include negative reactions toward the punisher, defensiveness, denial or disbelief, anger, disappointment, poor job attitudes, and less commitment to the organization. For example, Pence and Porter found that after negative performance appraisals, appraisal recipients had less commitment to the organization. They reported that they cared less about the organization's success and felt less willing to put in extra effort to help the organization succeed after receiving the negative appraisal.[8] A similar reaction may not result from negative feedback via a 360° intervention, but organizations should consider it a possibility. Perhaps the negative impact on commitment only occurs when the feedback is part of an evaluative, as opposed to developmental, process, or alternatively, if organizational support, such as training programs, is not offered to help the individual improve his or her behavior. Or perhaps the negative commitment in response to 360° feedback becomes targeted toward the rater(s) rather than the greater organization. These questions have yet to be answered by research.

How do companies maximize the positive impact of negative feedback and minimize the negative impact? In other words, how do they make the process shown in Exhibit 5-1 work? It is important that ratees perceive the feedback as honest and constructive. They will more likely accept the feedback as honest and accurate if convergence among sources, or within a source, exists. If the feedback recipient believes low scores resulted from only a few individuals who dislike him or her, the acceptance that some change may be needed is less likely. Companies should give feedback recipients time to digest the information and remind them that most individuals tend to overrate themselves. When the authors conduct feedback sessions in which 360° feedback results are presented, they ask individuals to work in pairs after receiving their feedback. The individuals are not expected to share numeric data, but rather to share their blindspots or areas in need of most improvement and to work together to identify strategies for change. This tends to reduce denial, improve acceptance, and promote the identification of strategies for improvement. Additionally, as mentioned in earlier chapters, at least in the beginning stages of a 360° feedback intervention, the purpose of the feedback should be for development, not evaluative decision making. Surveys of managers about their attitudes toward subordinate feedback suggested that the majority did not believe their companies should incorporate subordinates' ratings of them into their appraisals.[9] Indeed, these managers may have a point. While including subordinate ratings in a manager's appraisal could increase the manager's accountability to followers, some managers have suggested that they feared their behavior might be too driven toward getting good ratings from followers, perhaps at the expense of what was best for the department or organization. As mentioned in Chapter 3, certainly trade-offs surround the issue of using 360° feedback for development or evaluation.

Characteristics of the Feedback Recipient. Additional factors that impact whether ratees will accept the feedback as accurate or informative include characteristics of the feedback recipient, such as the recipient's level of self-esteem, gender, and age/tenure in the organization. Generally, those with high self-esteem feel less apprehensive about receiving feedback than those lacking self-esteem. Yet, feedback recipients with high self-esteem prefer positive feedback and will more likely accept the feedback if it confirms their positive self-perceptions. Those with high self-esteem also will likely rate themselves more highly than those without high self-esteem, even when their performance levels are the same. If high self-esteem individuals receive negative feedback that conflicts with their self-perceptions and degrees of self-esteem, they tend to place more credence in their own self-perceptions than in the ratings of others. While these individuals may be more receptive to the idea of feedback, if it disconfirms their self-perceptions, their high self-esteem makes it difficult to convince them that the negative feedback is warranted.

Those with low self-esteem, on the other hand, tend to take negative feedback more seriously and will even generalize the implications of the negative feedback to other aspects of their identities.[10] It is helpful if the coach providing the feedback and helping the recipient interpret it has some idea of the recipient's self-esteem. The coach can then counsel the recipient in a way to maximize the motivational effects of the feedback.

Regarding gender, women in general are more receptive to and influenced by others' evaluations of them than are men. Interestingly, this receptivity and acceptance does not stem from lower confidence, as researchers once thought, nor does it lead women to be more self-derogating. Rather, it reflects the tendency for females to consider the information more valuable than men do, which may lead them to more readily modify their behavior than men when weaknesses are pointed out.[11]

One of the reasons for this greater receptivity among females is that feedback may be more novel to females than males. As children and adolescents, boys tend to receive more evaluative feedback or attention, often in the form of criticism, from teachers and others than do girls. The feedback usually addresses conduct or behavior rather than abilities. As such, males become more desensitized to feedback and less influenced by it.[12] Alternatively, the classic male ego may come into play: Males may fear that acknowledging feedback that runs counter to their own inflated self-perception signifies weakness or insecurity.

Regarding age and tenure, older individuals and those who have worked in organizations longer tend to inflate their self-ratings compared with ratings they receive from others and tend to seek less feedback. Perhaps they believe they have received enough feedback, or perhaps they worry that others will see feedback seeking as a sign of insecurity; hence, they avoid it. As another possibility, the younger and less tenured employees may feel less certain about their abilities and thus more anxiously await feedback. Studies suggest that feedback seeking does *not* send a message of insecurity but rather enhances observers' impressions of the seeker, particularly if the feedback seeker generally performs well.[13] Regardless, neither age nor tenure seem to make individuals more responsive to feedback, nor do the years of experience appear to improve the accuracy of self-perception. Many times the more experienced managers seem to believe the 360° feedback process will not tell them anything they do not already know. They are often wrong!

What Should Follow Feedback?

Evidence suggests that it is not the feedback per se that has an impact on improvement, but rather the communication processes and goal setting that follow feedback prompt behavior change. Locke and Latham suggested that the developmental improvement goals set in response to feedback act as the primary determinants of behavior change.[14] Incorporating formal goal setting into the feedback process has great value. One company with whom the authors worked asked each manager to set development goals for improvement in their weak areas as identified in their feedback reports. The company then planned to include assessment of the extent to which managers met these goals as part of their next formal performance appraisals. Managers had the choice whether or not to use a Time 1/Time 2 comparison of two feedback scores as a measure of improvement. The scores would be compared over a specific time period. If the managers chose not to use the 360° results, they needed to specify some other measure they could use to demonstrate that they had achieved their goals.

Relatedly, David Antonioni found that those managers who met with the individuals who had provided the feedback after receiving their feedback results were most likely to realize improvements.[15] Of course, the managers most interested in self-improvement could have also been those most likely to seek additional feedback. Certainly, the averaged survey results provided in a feedback report, even if written comments are provided, are not as rich as face-to-face conversation. In a face-to-face group meeting, the feedback recipient can discuss development needs identified by the survey with subordinates, peers, managers, or customers. With the information provided in these discussions, the feedback recipient can develop more specific strategies for change. It is important, however, that feedback recipients do not attempt to discern who said what in these meetings, but rather they should embellish the survey information provided in the feedback report.

Organizational systems also critically impact whether individuals realize performance improvements. For example, what rewards are in place for individuals who make improvements? If 360° results indicate a supervisor needs to be more sensitive to employee concerns yet all rewards focus on bottom-line results that require large amounts of overtime to accomplish, the supervisor will have little incentive to attend to employee concerns.

Training provides another example. To what extent do the culture and budget support training for supervisors who need to develop soft skills? If supervisors need training to learn more-effective people-management techniques but such is unavailable, changes will be mediocre at best.

What Effects on Individual Outcomes Occur Over Time?

The extent to which an individual accepts and uses feedback can impact the accuracy of that individual's self-perception over time. Feedback from others or from the job itself regarding successful or unsuccessful accomplishment is critical for developing realistic job performance expectations. For example, those who underestimate their skills and abilities may set low aspiration levels, underachieve, and fail to pursue positions or tasks for which they are qualified. Overestimators fail to recognize needs for training and development, tend to blame others for their failures, and may have poor job attitudes because they believe companies undervalue them. Additionally, these overestimators will less likely be recommended for promotion and will more likely suffer from career derailment.[16] If 360° feedback provides these individuals with information about how others see them, they may have more realistic expectations about their abilities and be less likely to expect rewards they will probably not receive. If one's more realistic self-perception suggests promotion is unlikely, the individual probably will feel less disappointed and thus have better job attitudes when the promotion goes to another.

Results from several studies of upward and 360° feedback suggest that overestimators tend to lower their self-evaluations as a result of feedback, while underestimators tend to raise their self-evaluations.[17] If these self-evaluations reflect genuine changes in self-perception, they suggest that feedback may help individuals adopt more realistic self-perceptions over time, which in turn will lead to better career decisions. Whether or not changes in self-ratings actually have positive impacts on longer-term outcomes needs further study. Hazucha, Gentile, and Schneider found that after receiving feedback from subordinates, managers demonstrated increased skills, and those with greater skills were more likely to have advanced in the organization, suggesting that feedback can have an impact on longer-term outcomes.[18]

Further study is also needed to clearly determine the long-term impacts of feedback. For example, Jim Smither and colleagues[19] found that the most improvement from feedback came after the first feedback delivery and that future feedback sessions did not result in further improvements. However, would performance have declined had continued feedback not been given or had continued measurements not been taken? Because 360° feedback is relatively new and because a number of organizations have not continued to use it over time, long-term studies of its impact and continued use are few, and further research needs to be conducted.

At least some indications exist that suggest individuals can sustain the positive effects realized from feedback over time. Reilly, Smither, and Vasilopoulos demonstrated that managers who initially had low ratings from followers improved their performances after feedback and sustained this improvement for more than two years.[20] Additionally, as individuals continued to receive feedback over time, their self- and follower ratings continued to become more similar. However, interestingly, in this study those individuals who were rated by followers and *expected* to receive feedback but, because they had too few surveys returned, ultimately did not receive feedback, also realized improvements. Perhaps merely sensitizing one to desired behaviors and believing one will receive feedback can have as much impact on behavior change as actually receiving the feedback. Further research needs to take place to verify this conclusion.

IMPLICATIONS FOR THE FEEDBACK PROCESS

Feedback is necessary for individuals to develop realistic self-perceptions, and 360° feedback provides a more valid and comprehensive view of an individual's performance or behavior than feedback from one source, particularly when that source is not anonymous. However, the following characteristics of the feedback providers, recipients, and context can impact the quality of that feedback process:

1. If feedback recipients receive discrepant feedback from different sources, recipients tend to place more credence in positive ratings or ratings from sources who control outcomes. As such, those delivering feedback results need to alert recipients to this tendency and to steer them toward constructing action plans that address *each* source's assessments.

2. Individuals can have many reactions to their feedback, and as noted above, not all of these are positive or motivational. It is important that a neutral individual who has skill in feedback delivery provides feedback results if the maximum benefit is to be gained from the process. In other words, feedback reports should not simply be sent to recipients, but rather they should be delivered in a face-to-face session, either individually or in small groups.

3. Because negative feedback or unexpected low ratings are uncomfortable, individuals may attempt to minimize the discomfort by making changes, or improvements, in their behaviors. It is therefore important that companies make methods for skill development, such as training, available to individuals desiring such. For example,

if an individual scores low on his or her ability to successfully resolve conflict, training in conflict resolution may be indicated. Companies should encourage feedback recipients to pursue additional training or counseling as needed and should make resources available for this purpose.

4. Valid ratings are important if the feedback process is to succeed. This means that companies should solicit the best sources of information to provide information on specific topics. For example, managers who rarely interact with employees will not be in the best position to rate those individuals' interpersonal skills. Likewise, the extent to which the ratee acts as a coach or mentor to followers is best rated by followers. Oftentimes, organizations adopt a one-size-fits-all approach to survey design, in which many sources rate the same aspects of performance. This is efficient and allows comparisons across rater groups, but feedback recipients need to identify individuals in the best positions to provide accurate ratings of each skill and to stress those ratings when interpreting their feedback.

5. In most cases, descriptive or behavioral feedback is more useful than evaluative feedback. For example, if the survey asks an individual to rate how often the supervisor listens attentively to the ideas of others, the information is more useful than if the survey merely asks the rater to evaluate the supervisor's listening skills. As such, ratings of specific behaviors are most useful.

6. Feedback works best when follow-up with feedback providers, goal setting, and accountability for change are included. Accordingly, companies should encourage supervisors to help feedback recipients acquire additional feedback and develop improvement plans. Supervisors should do this without focusing on scores from the feedback report but rather in general terms about how recipients could make and measure improvements in a particular area.

7. Organizational systems such as rewards and training need to align with the behaviors targeted in the 360° instrument in order for the 360° process to produce the most benefit.

8. Changing self-perception comes easier if it is not firmly entrenched. Therefore, it is important to do 360° feedback early in an individual's career. It also helps if individuals receive feedback before they have developed habits and styles that become more difficult to change over time.

9. Anonymity of ratings is important in order to receive the most candid ratings, particularly from peers and subordinates. Companies should allow *all* subordinates or peer group members to complete surveys rather than allowing the ratee to select his or her own raters. Some 360° feedback providers limit the number of raters per ratee or have the raters distribute surveys to those individuals they believe can best rate them. Often companies do this for expedience rather than to maximize the usefulness of the feedback. However, particularly in the case of subordinates, supervisors should survey *all* subordinates. This gives everyone an opportunity to participate if they choose and maximizes the reliability and validity of the data. When supervisors select subordinates to rate them, they may select raters with whom they agree or get along, and thus they may receive artificially high ratings. In addition, those not selected to do the ratings may feel slighted. In cases where the number of peers or customers is very large, some companies ask the ratee to select a list of raters, and the ratee's supervisor must approve this list. This approval process is included to encourage ratees to select a representative sample of raters, rather than a set of friends.

10. Age, tenure, or experience do not contribute to more accurate self-appraisals, and companies should not consider these as substitutes for 360° feedback. While more experienced individuals may not believe 360° feedback will tell them anything they do not already know, research evidence suggests these individuals tend to have less accurate self-perceptions, perhaps because they seek less feedback. So, organizations should encourage 360° feedback at all levels of experience and hierarchy.

SUMMARY

This chapter has addressed the ways self-awareness can impact individual outcomes and the importance of feedback in the development of self-awareness. The relevance of various individual characteristics to feedback receptivity and use has also been discussed. The next chapter takes a broader view of the impact of 360° feedback on organizations. Specifically, it addresses the relationship between 360° feedback initiatives and organizational culture.

REFERENCES

1. See S. Ashford and A. Tsui, "Self-regulation for Managerial Effectiveness: The Role of Active Feedback Seeking," *Academy of Management Journal,* 34 (1991), p. 254.

2. See A. Kluger and A. DeNisi, "The Effects of Feedback Interventions on Performance: A Historical Review, A Meta-analysis, and a Preliminary Feedback Intervention Theory," *Psychological Bulletin,* 119 (1996), pp. 254–284.

3. See J. Smither, et al., "An Examination of the Effects of an Upward Feedback Program Over Time," *Personnel Psychology,* 48, (1995), pp. 1–33.

4. See L. Atwater, P. Roush, and A. Fischthal, "The Influence of Upward Feedback on Self- and Follower Ratings of Leadership," *Personnel Psychology,* 48 (1995), pp. 35–59.

5. See M. Harris and J. Schaubroeck, "A Meta-analysis of Self-Supervisor, Self-Peer, and Peer-Supervisor Ratings," *Personnel Psychology,* 41 (1988), pp. 43–62.

6. See M. London and A. Wohlers, "Agreement Between Subordinates and Self-ratings in Upward Feedback," *Personnel Psychology,* 44 (1991), pp. 375–390.

7. J. Bernardin, S. Dahmus, and G. Redmon, "Attitudes of First-Line Supervisors Toward Subordinate Appraisal," *Human Resource Management,* 32 (1993), pp. 315–324.

8. See J. Pence and L. Porter, "Employee Responses to Formal Performance Appraisal Feedback," *Journal of Applied Psychology,* 71 (1986), pp. 211–218.

9. D. Antonioni, "The Effects of Feedback Accountability on Upward Appraisal," *Personnel Psychology,* 47 (1994), pp. 349–356.

10. M. Kernis, J. Brockner, and B. Frankel, "Self-esteem and Reactions to Failure: The Mediating Role of Overgeneralization," *Journal of Personality and Social Psychology,* 57 (1989), pp. 707–714.

11. See T. Roberts and S. Nolen-Hoeksema, "Gender Comparisons in Responsiveness to Others' Evaluations in Achievement Settings," *Psychology of Women Quarterly,* 18 (1994), pp. 221–240.

12. Ibid.

13. See S. Ashford and A. Tsui, "Self-regulation for Managerial Effectiveness. The Role of Active Feedback Seeking," *Academy of Management Journal,* 34 (1991), pp. 251–280.

14. E. Locke and G. Latham, *A Theory of Goal-Setting and Task Performance* (Englewood Cliffs, N.J.: Prentice-Hall, 1990).

15. D. Antonioni, "Designing an Effective 360-Degree Appraisal Feedback Process," *Organizational Dynamics,* 25 (1996), pp. 24–38.

16. See:

L. Atwater and F. Yammarino, "Does Self-Other Agreement on Leadership Perceptions Moderate the Validity of Leadership and Performance Predictions?" *Personnel Psychology,* 45 (1992), pp. 141–164.

E. Van Velsor, S. Taylor, and J. Leslie, "An Examination of the Relationship Between Self-perception Accuracy, Self-awareness, and Gender and Leader Effectiveness," *Human Resource Management,* 32 (1992), pp. 249–264.

17. Atwater, Roush, and Fischthal, op cit.

18. J. Hazucha, S. Gentile, and R. Schneider, "Impact of 360-Degree Feedback on Management Skills Development," (Working paper, Personnel Decisions Inc., 1993).

19. Smither, et al., op cit.

20. R. Reilly, J. Smither, and N. Vasilopoulos, "A Longitudinal Study of Upward Feedback," *Personnel Psychology,* 49 (1996), pp. 599–612.

CHAPTER 6

What Is the Connection to Organizational Culture?

One reason for the popularity of 360° feedback is that its proponents claim implementation can have positive effects on the culture of an organization. This chapter will explore the connection between 360° feedback and organizational culture and will begin by carefully defining culture in an organizational context. In so doing, this chapter will consider a popular form of culture in recent times that has become associated with the phenomenon of total quality. The relationship between 360° feedback and a total quality culture will be clarified. This discussion will then lead into an elaboration of the push-pull relationship between 360° feedback and organizational culture, an issue introduced in Chapter 2. This chapter concludes with an acknowledgment of the potential downside of 360° feedback with regard to culture, that is, the potential for negative effects.

Defining Organizational Culture

Culture can be defined as a set of underlying assumptions, beliefs, values, and norms shared within a group of people that guides the group's perceptions and overt behaviors. Culture can be considered at various levels of analysis. For example, one can think of a distinctly American culture. One can also envision regional cultures, such as the northeastern portion of the United States versus its southern or western portions. In addition, culture has been conceived at the corporate or organizational level. In other words, people associate unique cultures with organizations, for example IBM versus Apple.

Organizational culture has been described as playing a strong role in shaping behaviors, ideologies, and policies of organizations.[1] Yet, to many people, culture remains a mysterious phenomenon because a person cannot see or touch it, unlike other organizational phenomena, such as organizational charts, policy manuals, and layout of office space. At the same time, most managers and many researchers would acknowledge the potential of culture to affect a company's performance. This text takes that view but also contends that to truly understand the power of culture and its relationship to 360° feedback, one must delineate a relevant framework. Total quality provides one such logical framework, pursued here.

The Total Quality Culture

While providing a universally accepted definition of total quality (TQ) proves difficult, a number of themes have emerged during the past ten to fifteen years.[2] These include:

1. An emphasis on quality as a management strategy, with a special focus on quality as perceived through the eyes of customers;
2. Upper-management commitment to place quality as a top priority;
3. The development of leadership throughout all levels of management;
4. Cooperative behavior within groups and between functional areas, or teamwork;
5. Involvement of every organizational member in quality improvement efforts, not just quality control specialists or customer service representatives;

6. Attempts to get external suppliers and customers involved in TQ efforts;

7. Enhanced organizational communication and feedback systems; and

8. Frequent use of scientific and problem-solving techniques to solve problems and continually improve quality.

As one can see, these themes fit nicely with the definition of culture provided earlier. In other words, TQ largely represents a cultural phenomenon, as well as a business strategy.[3] Indeed, to think of TQ as merely a set of technical or statistical innovations would, in all likelihood, create a recipe for disaster when attempting implementation. An interesting study conducted in the late 1980s demonstrated specifically how the more technical aspects of TQ implementation, such as statistical process control, are not likely to be successfully deployed unless key aspects of cultural change are simultaneously taken into account.[4] In addition, a recent study demonstrated how leadership and cultural factors predicted the success of TQ initiatives more than technical factors, such as those related to process improvements and statistical methodology.[5]

Total Quality Culture and 360° Feedback

The connection between a TQ culture and 360° feedback processes should be apparent. A number of commonalities exist. First, TQ stresses the development of leadership. As argued in the previous chapter, people best develop leadership qualities through the type of self-awareness that a 360° feedback process, especially upward feedback, can derive. The information gleaned by managers can prove useful as input to developmental planning specifically geared toward the improvement of leadership skills and behaviors.

Second, in a similar manner, 360° information supplied by peers can give individuals a better awareness of how they contribute to team efforts, both within and between teams. Without such information, teamwork will less likely occur given the individualistic orientation of American society.[6] The mere act of measuring teamwork-oriented behavior through peer appraisals and then feeding the information back to individuals sends a strong message about the value of teamwork within the organization's culture.

Third, both upward and peer appraisals represent means of demonstrating employee involvement. For years, practitioners and academics alike have sung the praises of employee involvement. Survey/feedback programs in general and 360° feedback in particular have proved useful mechanisms for getting employees involved. Employees' senses of involvement are perhaps especially strong when asked to provide upward feedback about their bosses. This is demonstrated by the generally high response rates obtained when companies ask subordinates to rate superiors, even when subordinates respond through the use of anonymous, mailout procedures.

Fourth, peer and upward feedback provide a mechanism by which internal customers, that is coworkers and subordinates, can report the extent to which their needs are being met. Although less often surveyed in 360° feedback programs, external customers can also provide feedback to organizational members with regard to services provided. However, as mentioned earlier, it may prove difficult to focus customer feedback toward particular employees, as is typically the case with 360° feedback. Customers oftentimes have minimal contact with any one employee. Nevertheless, internal customers can provide useful individual information in many cases.

In general, 360° feedback initiatives provide a concrete means of enhancing organizational communication and feedback systems and ensuring the maximum involvement of internal and external customers, or raters, as well as suppliers, or ratees, in TQ efforts. As the net effect, TQ becomes consistent with the notion of "boundaryless organization."[7] In recent years, many organizations have attempted to become more boundaryless by maintaining flatter structures and allowing a more free flow of communication and influence with customers and suppliers. Such strategies have led to closer customer-supplier relationships. The extent to which an organization has attempted to reshape its boundaries structurally toward boundarylessness coincides with the appropriateness of 360° degree feedback. For example, a flatter structure would increase the need for upward appraisals and feedback, as managers attempt to gauge the effectiveness of their leadership behaviors. As the span of control increases and rigid control systems become less applicable, any individual manager is less likely to have enough relevant information about his or her employees' performances to provide meaningful appraisals. Additional information can be gleaned potentially from subordinates, peers, customers, and so forth.

As another example, a boundaryless organization might encourage the contracting of services across functional or product-line boundaries. With such contracting comes closer contact and the natural development of customer-supplier relationships between previously separated groups. One specific example increasingly common in recent years involves the contracting of human resource services between an HR department and other units of an organization. The message to the HR department is that it, as the supplier, is accountable for meeting the HR needs of internal customers. The use of 360° feedback would likely seem appropriate to both customers and the HR supplier in such a context.

The breaking down of boundaries between an organization and its external customers has caused those customers to take a more active role toward the organization and its management. For example, in service settings that have adopted boundaryless orientations, external customers increasingly become more involved in the design and delivery of the company's HRM practices. Southwest Airlines invites frequent passengers to serve on interviewer panels, screening applicants for flight attendants' positions. In other words, Southwest Airlines gives these passengers a voice in hiring decisions.[8] Customers who participate in such a boundaryless context could also be expected to willingly provide 360° feedback, again assuming such feedback makes sense at the individual level.

WHAT'S DRIVING WHAT?

The relationship between 360° feedback processes and organizational culture provides an interesting study in the old chicken-and-egg dilemma of which comes first. Does an organization implement 360° feedback to have a positive impact on cultural change? Chapter 2 referred to this as the *push* phenomenon. Or alternatively, is an organization that already possesses a culture that stresses change, innovation, and trust simply likely to adopt 360° feedback processes? Chapter 2 referred to this as the *pull* phenomenon.

These questions become important if one wants to form an in-depth understanding of how 360° feedback can impact organizations and whether such efforts will likely achieve success. In Chapter 3, the interviews with several HR professionals who had implemented 360° feedback pointed out that it is important to consider how such efforts fit within the larger organizational context and change processes. Specifically, these HR professionals readily described what they perceived to be the connection between 360° feedback and organizational culture. For example, one person noted how 360° feedback models new values for an organization.

Another mentioned how by simply having such a program, a company sends a strong message that the culture is becoming more participative.

These examples illustrate the *push* phenomenon, which represents the most common reason organizations pursue 360° feedback. Specifically, organizations take interest in using it as a mechanism to change the organizational culture—more toward one conducive to change, innovation, and TQ. Such a motive makes sense and, indeed, represents a plausible reason for pursuing 360° feedback implementation.

At the same time, the *push* motive does not automatically guarantee success. Indeed, organizations do not easily or quickly accomplish culture change. Success depends on previous management innovation efforts and current management resolve. Emotions tend to heighten greatly when an organization uses a 360° feedback program as part of a companywide change effort. These emotions may give way to anxiety, suspicion, and even paranoia, especially when memories of previously failed or dropped change efforts surface.

A recent experience of the authors with a state policing organization provides an interesting example of the *push* phenomenon at work. They worked closely with the agency to implement upward feedback in an attempt to *push* the traditional, quasi-military culture toward one that encourages participation from all levels. This process began with the director of the agency implementing upward feedback for himself and his staff. The director also conducted a feedback session with his subordinates after receiving his feedback report. The authors facilitated that feedback session. The director opened the discussion by identifying the areas that the report said needed development. The director then left the room, and the authors solicited specific suggestions from subordinates as to how the director could improve. The outside facilitation was used in this case because the director feared that his subordinates might be reluctant to make suggestions directly to him. Once these were identified, the group presented the suggestions to the director.

One month after the introduction of the feedback, a number of the agency director's immediate subordinates reported that they had witnessed a noticeable improvement in the director's management behaviors. They attributed this to the upward feedback he received. As this type of change is witnessed at the top levels and trickles down, and as the organization implements upward feedback at lower levels, the *push* toward culture change will begin. Thus, one will begin to see a connection between individual and cultural change.

Exhibit 6-1 shows a model depicting the *push* phenomenon and its potential for successful impact on culture. The section below describes the model and its components in detail.

Desires Behind the *Push*

The model shows how several rational desires can *push* a 360° feedback implementation effort. First, a desire for more and/or better leadership practices may exist. This desire has been a key driver of the proliferation of 360° feedback and the reason why so many efforts have focused on upward feedback. The implicit notion is that subordinates occupy the best positions to observe and evaluate leadership practices and are thus logical choices to provide such feedback to people in leadership roles.

Second, a desire may exist for the organization's culture to stress teamwork as a value and norm of behavior. A lack of teamwork and associated internal competition or fiefdom building can create noncooperation in organizations and result in low quality, slow response time, and lack of innovation.[9] Peer feedback, another form or direction of 360° feedback, has been viewed as a means of clarifying to peers the extent to which team-oriented behavior occurs.

Curiously, to the best of the authors' knowledge, most peer feedback efforts have focused on peers within intact work groups, that is, they have been targeted at within-group teamwork. Organizations have devoted less energy to obtaining peer feedback across workgroups, or what may be referred to as internal customer feedback. Perhaps this illustrates the fiefdom mentality that persists in organizations. Alternatively, given the individualized orientation of 360° feedback, those responsible for implementation may simply not view internal customer feedback across groups as highly feasible or appropriate. Also, most off-the-shelf instruments may not address aspects of behavior that internal customers can validly rate. Or like external customer feedback, feedback from individuals in other departments may only make sense when delivered to a group of individuals. Examples include feedback from a group in charge of production to a group in charge of product design, feedback from a group in charge of sales to a group involved in market research, and so forth.

The desire to enhance employee involvement fits together neatly with 360° feedback implementation efforts. Employee involvement and empowerment have long been touted as vital components of organizational effectiveness.[10] What can companies do to make employees feel more involved and empowered? A number of possibilities come to mind, including:

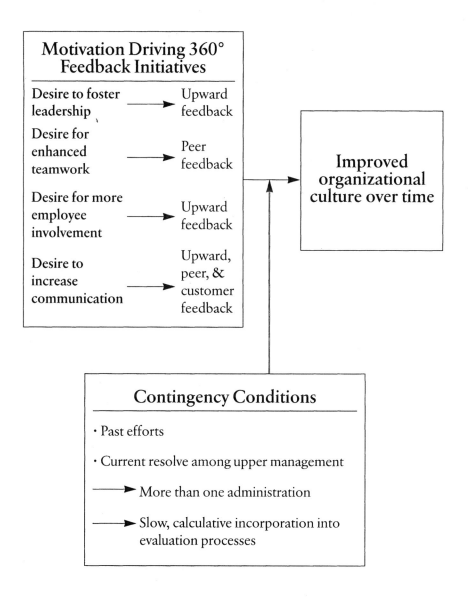

Exhibit 6-1. 360° Feedback Pushing Organizational Culture

1. Active search for employee input into decision-making processes;

2. Employee suggestion programs;

3. Delegation of *both* responsibility and authority to employees;

4. Semiautonomous team structures; and

5. Survey/feedback programs.

Among these approaches, 360° feedback most obviously relates to traditional survey/feedback. The difference lies in the nature of the feedback target. Survey/feedback programs typically target job and organizational-level phenomena, such as job conditions and human resource policies. In contrast, 360° feedback obviously focuses on individuals. By providing a mechanism for peers and subordinates to provide behavioral feedback, 360° feedback becomes a tool for employee involvement. It also becomes an empowerment tool, giving employees a chance to influence the developmental planning, and even the evaluation, of others.

However, one caveat is necessary. Traditional, survey/feedback only proves effective when those surveyed believe the company will indeed use the data for some beneficial purpose. For 360° feedback to become such a mechanism, peers and subordinates who provide the data need to see follow-up actions. Such actions could include follow-up sessions with raters to obtain further feedback and clarification of data provided to the ratee in a feedback report. Developmental action planning and noticeable change on the part of a ratee and further opportunities for providing feedback at later times also enhance a sense of empowerment on the part of raters.

A final factor *pushing* organizations toward the implementation of 360° feedback programs involves the desire to increase communication. Ineffective or inappropriate behaviors, especially on the part of management, can stifle attempts of organizations to continuously improve processes and quality and to increase flexibility. Feedback is an essential mechanism to identify problematic behavior. Unfortunately, traditional top-down feedback, such as performance appraisal feedback, provides only one perspective and can include leniency biases. That is, a supervisor may not know of a respective subordinate's poor teamwork or poor leadership behaviors; conversely, peers and subordinates of that individual can provide more accurate insights. In addition, supervisory feedback is not anonymous and will likely come attached to evaluative processes, such as a performance appraisal report. Accordingly, supervisors may feel reluctant to provide negative feedback because it could affect working relationships and damage a subordinate's personnel record. In short, 360° feedback provides a broader perspective and, because of its anonymity, could provide more accurate behavioral feedback to targeted ratees.

Contingency Conditions

Does 360° feedback inevitably lead to an improved organizational culture? Although intuition might suggest a positive answer, as shown in Exhibit 6-1, a more prudent response is, "Maybe, but it depends." In essence, it depends on two factors: (1) The nature of past initiatives directed toward organizational change; and (2) current resolve among management.

"It's the flavor of the month. Let's hold our breath, and maybe this one will go away soon." Unfortunately, such cynical attitudes pervade organizations in current times—perhaps for good reason. As noted in Chapter 3, organizations do not always implement initiatives directed toward change in a consistent, long-term manner. Instead, organizational members become excited by new initiatives, for example, quality improvement and process reengineering. Their excitement leads to attempts at changing behaviors and methods used to accomplish work. Change for most humans is a stressful phenomenon. It becomes even more stressful when the organization does not carry out the change to a logical conclusion or a point where homeostasis can be reached.

Such is the case for many individuals subjected to change initiatives who quickly find the rug pulled out from under them. That is, managers change their minds or are replaced or transferred, and/or budgets and resources for the new initiative get cut, and the change initiative goes away. Disillusionment occurs because organizational members may feel betrayed. After all, they had gone through the stress of unfreezing their behaviors or work . methods, only to learn it was all for naught. As the upshot, the next time management gets the urge to engage in a new initiative, people tend to characterize it cynically as the flavor of the month, and garnering their support becomes difficult.

Current management cannot erase the past. However, it can acknowledge past implementation mistakes pertaining to change initiatives and show resolve with regard to new initiatives, such as 360° feedback. One simple way to show resolve is to allow for more than one administration of a 360° process. It is ill-advised to ask a ratee to go through a 360° administration and receive feedback—some of which may be surprisingly negative and unpleasant—and then not give the ratee a chance to demonstrate improvement. The ratee needs to have a second chance, or perhaps several chances, to show improved results. By demonstrating such resolve, management can thwart potential disillusionment and can realize the cultural improvements that 360° feedback implementation can offer.

Companies can also show resolve by effectively treading the fine line by incorporating 360° data into developmental planning while not using such data as an evaluation stick. Chapter 3 mentioned an upward feedback pilot project the authors implemented at a large telecommunication company. A high-level manager in charge of one of the units targeted for the project wanted to immediately use the data in an evaluative manner. In other words, he wanted the data made available to the supervisors of respective ratees so the supervisors could base job transfers, demotions/promotions, and so forth on the data.

The authors successfully persuaded him that such a strategy would tear down, rather than benefit, the culture. Specifically, it would have spread fear and distrust among targeted ratees. In addition, game playing would have probably ensued whereby ratees and raters, or subordinates, would make implicit and even explicit deals to ensure mutually beneficial outcomes. For example, ratees might assure subordinates that if they provide "fair" ratings with regard to the upward feedback, that the ratees would, in turn, give them "fair" performance appraisals at the end of the year. In short, this would not have resulted in improvements in the company's culture.

On the other hand, companies need to incorporate some degree of accountability early on. A total lack of accountability would result in little cultural improvement for two reasons. First, ratees would have less motivation to use the feedback to make behavioral improvements. Second, if raters see no action taken as a result of a 360° feedback effort, they will become disillusioned and feel that the organization's attempt to involve them had no real credibility.

In the telecommunication example, the authors suggested ratees identify three or four specific behavioral areas in need of improvement and set developmental goals in conjunction with their bosses. The bosses would not see the ratings per se but would still begin to hold the ratees accountable for making improvements over time. Depending on the degree of trust that builds over time, subsequent administrations could increasingly become evaluative in nature, especially in terms of redirecting the career paths of those who continue to score especially low.

360° FEEDBACK: ALONG FOR THE RIDE?

While the *push* phenomenon provides a likely explanation for the connection between 360° feedback and culture, many situations exist in which an established culture simply *pulls* a 360° feedback initiative along. In other words, the culture of the organization has progressed to the point of naturally absorbing innovations like 360° feedback. Such a culture stresses openness of communication, trust, innovation, and lack of cynicism regarding change efforts. Not surprisingly, such a cultural evolution would also prove quite conducive to absorbing the cultural values, beliefs, and norms associated with total quality. That is, a culture with such basic elements could readily adopt values, beliefs, and norms stressing continuous improvement, internal and external customer-supplier relationships, teamwork, and the need for effective leadership.

Organizations of this type routinely scan the external environment in search of technological and managerial innovations. When an innovation like 360° feedback appears on the radar screen, the organization makes efforts to benchmark best practices. Adoption becomes a relatively smooth process because the 360° feedback fits in neatly with the existing culture, only reinforcing it further. Exhibit 6-2 shows a model of the mutual reinforcing of a *pull* culture and 360° feedback.

Chapter 3 noted a case example of a high-tech computer company whose culture was *pulled* along by 360° feedback. Because of established levels of trust in the culture, feedback information was sent not only to targeted ratees, but also to their bosses. Raters did not fear retribution, and the company assured managers, or ratees, that even if it used the data evaluatively, for example, as part of promotion decisions, the company would treat them fairly. In contrast, employees in a company experiencing the *push* phenomenon, that is, 360° feedback being used to *push* the culture toward improvement, would likely feel leery of such practices. They would feel suspicious of their supervisors receiving reports of their ratings and would often believe the supervisors would not use such reports fairly for evaluative purposes.

In short, it appears that the ideal situation is for 360° feedback to simply be absorbed by an existing organizational culture that is ready, willing, and able to do so. One reinforces the other. Unfortunately, this is often not the case, and instead companies employ a riskier strategy of using 360° feedback to *push* a culture in new directions. The next chapter will say more about these issues when it attempts to form the linkage between 360° feedback and organizational performance. The remainder of this chapter will consider the potential downside of 360° feedback in relation to culture.

IS THERE A POTENTIAL FOR NEGATIVE EFFECTS ON CULTURE?

At first glimpse, this question might appear puzzling. Indeed, so far this chapter has made a strong argument for the positive effects of 360° feedback on organizational cultures. Such things as leadership, teamwork, employee involvement and empowerment, and communication can all be enhanced. So what could create a possible downside? Three factors deserve consideration:

1. Bad feedback;
2. Poor motives and commitment on the part of raters; and
3. Overly evaluative usages.

Bad Feedback

No guarantees exist that, when provided the opportunity, raters in a 360° feedback process will provide good feedback. Feedback that lacks quality cannot benefit the recipients and, thus, will less likely benefit the greater organizational culture. So what exactly is good feedback? It does not refer to necessarily positive feedback. Somewhat critical feedback can prove quite beneficial to the feedback recipient. Indeed, people can learn as much or more from critical feedback as from positive feedback.

Bad feedback has several characteristics. First, the actual ratings are fraught with rating errors, such as central tendency, or using only the middle values of the rating scale; leniency, which can be both positive and negative; and halo. Second, the ratings contain biases, such as the game playing that can occur when 360° feedback is highly evaluative within a culture lacking trust. In both these cases, this inaccurate feedback can be worse than no feedback. Third, the feedback provided in a 360° process can be somewhat qualitative in nature, especially if surveys involve write-in comments. Such comments do not help if provided in very general terms. Examples include such generalized descriptors as *lazy, lacking credibility, arrogant,* and *obnoxious.* Individuals require more specific behavioral

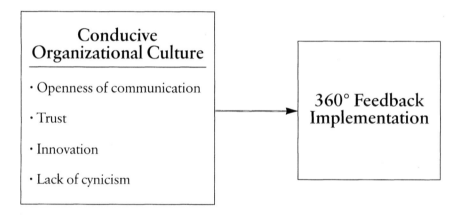

Exhibit 6-2. Organizational Culture Pulling 360° Feedback Along

feedback including examples if they are to change. Even positive general-ized descriptors may not provide helpful feedback. Examples include *good leader, team player,* and *good communicator.* To maintain these qualities, specific behavioral feedback would help. This feedback is not necessarily harmful, just not very useful. Bad feedback can also stem from bad survey items that are too general or given to raters unfamiliar with a ratee's behav-ior in the areas being rated.

Bad feedback probably occurs more often in a 360° process, compared with the more traditional feedback processes that occur when supervisors provide feedback to subordinates as part of normal performance appraisals. This is not to say that all supervisors provide feedback like experts. However, they may have more experience than many individuals called upon to be raters in a 360° feedback process. For example, nonman-agerial subordinates who provide upward feedback may have never had prior opportunities to rate the behavior of another individual. No one should be surprised if bad feedback results. A paper by G. Greguras and C. Robie presented at the 1997 meeting of the Society for Industrial and Organizational Psychology in St. Louis demonstrated that supervisor rat-ings provided on a 360° instrument had more reliability than peer ratings and that peer ratings had more reliability than subordinate ratings. Supervi-sor ratings also relate more strongly to objective aspects of job perfor-mance, as compared with peer ratings.[11]

The obvious solution to the bad-feedback problem is to properly inform 360° raters of the purpose of their ratings. In addition, they should receive proper training in how to form ratings, for example, how to avoid rating errors, and how to write behavioral feedback in write-in comments. Obvi-ously, such training could cost a lot of money since, by definition, 360° feedback involves many raters. However, two goals can be accomplished by utilizing information sessions prior to 360° administrations. During these sessions, raters can learn the purpose of the 360° program, as well as obtain training in rating processes.

Poor Motives and Commitment

Chapter 4 mentioned potential problems academicians face because of the strong emphasis frequently placed on student evaluations of teaching effectiveness. While students can provide useful information when evaluat-ing their teachers and courses, they also tend to approach the situation with short-term, narrowly focused motives. Specifically, they oftentimes seek a smooth, comfortable learning experience involving an entertaining environment and accountability for learning placed in the hands of instructors, rather than students.

Similar situations can occur in industry. For example, in the case of upward feedback, many managers might worry that allowing for such input is akin to allowing the monkeys to run the zoo. Such ideas are extreme, and indeed, these managers would probably be skeptical of other methods of employee involvement or empowerment.

At the same time, employees driven by self-serving motives and a lack of commitment to organizational goals may not make good candidates to provide upward feedback ratings. They might provide low upward feedback ratings to their managers simply because those managers have high performance expectations and refuse to cater to the desires of whiny employees. Alternatively, these employees may give low ratings because they see their managers as devoting too much time to external customers.

To be sure, in a 360° framework, subordinates are also considered customers, albeit internal customers. However, in this case the customers may not always be right, especially when taking into account that their needs may run counter to adhering to the needs of external customers. An overemphasis on upward ratings might cause managers to have lower performance expectations and attach less value to meeting the needs of external customers. The net result would not benefit the organization's culture.

Overly Evaluative Usage

Once again the thorny issue of evaluation surfaces. The problems mentioned above are accentuated when evaluative usages are attached to a 360° feedback process, especially in an organizational culture already experiencing problems associated with lack of trust and cynicism. Catering to the self-serving needs of some peers or subordinates, even at the expense of other internal and external customers and greater organizational goals, only becomes a problem when 360° processes become too evaluative too quickly.

As suggested consistently throughout this book, the solution in most circumstances is to move in the direction of evaluation only in a deliberate manner. Indeed, rarely should companies emphasize playing a numbers game, that is, establishing a situation where ratees compete for slightly higher ratings for the purposes of obtaining pay raises, promotions, and so forth. If used at all for evaluative purposes, companies should only identify those ratees with scores that consistently remain at unacceptable levels, even after repeated administrations.

SUMMARY AND CONCLUSIONS

This chapter began with an assumption that a strong connection exists between the implementation of 360° feedback programs and organizational culture. Along these lines, the chapter clarified the linkage between 360° feedback and total quality. It also went into detail with regard to both the *push* and the *pull* phenomena that can characterize the connection between 360° feedback and culture. The *push* phenomenon probably occurs most frequently and represents a desire on the part of organizations to use 360° feedback to effect positive cultural change. Alternatively, the *pull* phenomenon occurs when a relatively healthy organization simply uses such a program as a natural continuation or reinforcement of its existing culture. This chapter spent time considering the contingency factors that determine whether organizations can successfully use 360° feedback to help *push* themselves toward positive cultural change.

The text also considered the potential downside of 360° feedback with regard to cultural change. Indeed, many prior proponents of 360° feedback have failed to consider potential negative consequences. However, it is important for organizations to approach such initiatives carefully, including a realization of the various factors that can cause organizations to go awry and actually do damage to their cultures. To this extent, the chapter offered a number of suggestions and recommendations.

The next chapter turns attention to the real bottom line—organizational performance. Not surprisingly, forming the connection between 360° feedback initiatives and organizational performance is not an easy or clear task. It nevertheless is an important consideration if 360° feedback is to continue to flourish. By first addressing organizational culture, this book has attempted to set the stage for a consideration of performance outcomes.

REFERENCES

1. For in-depth discussions of the role of culture in shaping organizational behavior, see:

T. Deal and A. Kennedy, *Corporate Cultures* (Reading, Mass.: Addison-Wesley, 1982).

E. H. Schein, "Organizational Culture," *American Psychologist,* 45 (1990), pp. 109–119.

2. Adapted from D. A. Waldman, "A Theoretical Consideration of Leadership and Total Quality Management," *Leadership Quarterly*, 4 (1993), pp. 65–79.

3. For a detailed consideration of total quality as both cultural phenomenon and a business strategy, see J. W. Dean, Jr., and J. Evans, *Total Quality: Management, Organization, and Strategy* (St. Paul: West, 1994).

4. The reference for that study is G. R. Bushe, "Cultural Contradictions of Statistical Process Control in American Manufacturing Organizations," *Journal of Management,* 14 (1988), pp. 19–31.

5. See T. C. Powell, "Total Quality Management as Competitive Advantage: A Review and Empirical Study," *Strategic Management Journal,* 16 (1995), pp. 15–37.

6. The individualistic tendency of American society is portrayed in Nancy Adler's book, *International Dimensions of Organizational Behavior,* 3rd ed. (Cincinnati: South-Western College Publishing, 1997).

7. The concept of boundaryless organization was explained by the following book: R. Ashkenas, et al., *The Boundaryless Organization* (San Francisco: Jossey-Bass, 1995).

8. The authors are indebted to David Bowen for providing this example.

9. For a discussion of a holistic, as opposed to segmented, organization, see:
Bushe, op cit.
Dean and Evans, op cit.

10. As an example, see E. E. Lawler, *High-Involvement Management: Participative Strategies for Improving Organizational Performance* (San Francisco: Jossey-Bass, 1986).

11. See C. Viswesvaran, "Modeling Job Performance: So There Is a General Factor?" Doctoral Dissertation, University of Iowa, 1996.

CHAPTER 7

Does 360° Feedback Impact Organizational Performance?

This chapter deals with the toughest issue faced in this book. Yet, a book that claims to examine the impact of 360° feedback on organizations must face this topic. The bad news is that little if any available systematic research evidence addresses this issue. That is, research simply has not been completed that systematically examines whether 360° feedback initiatives can, in and of themselves, affect organizational performance.

The good news is that a growing area of related research and theory suggests that human resource strategies and practices, in general, can indeed make a significant difference to a firm's bottom line. The challenge lies in showing how 360° feedback in particular can result in economic, and related, benefits. To do so, this chapter will borrow from existing literature to develop a practical model of performance effects. Before building that model, one must consider the following: What exactly does *organizational performance* mean?

Organizational Performance

Financial measures often constitute conceptualizations of organizational performance. For example, people commonly think of such indices as return on investment, return on equity, earnings per share, sales growth, and the like.[1]

Organizations represent a broad group of stakeholders and groups involved in defining and affecting performance. Accordingly, one should broaden definitions of organizational performance to include a larger domain that encompasses more operational indices. For example, one might consider market share, rate of new product or service introduction, product/service quality, measures of technological efficiency, and so forth.

One problem in attempting to link 360° feedback with organizational performance is that a multitude of factors can cause organizations to perform successfully, or conversely, to fail. Indeed, this issue makes it difficult to connect any particular management initiatives or strategies to performance. Macro factors pertaining to the greater economy can affect performance, for example, the general state of the economy. Alternatively, a variety of technological circumstances, such as the introduction of new machinery, and social circumstances, such as labor/management relations, can affect performance. Consequently, teasing out cause-and-effect relationships can prove messy in the real world of organizations.

With this in mind, one should consider broader operational measures in the realm of 360° feedback initiatives. Financial measures are further removed and, thus, more difficult to connect directly to 360° feedback. This does not mean such connections cannot be made, only that because of the multitude of other factors affecting financial indices, making an unequivocal linkage is tenuous at best. On the other hand, the connection between 360° feedback and more operational measures may be a bit cleaner.

A tangible example may help. A company might find that the quality of services has fallen, at least in the eyes of customers. It appears that much of the problem lies in a lack of coordinated effort on the part of various groups of employees and managers to understand and serve the needs of external customers. The company undertakes a 360° feedback initiative, and the improved communication that results eventually translates into enhanced service quality—an operational measure of performance. Enhanced service quality could then translate into improved market share—another measure of operational performance. Of course, such improvement assumes that competitors do not also use 360° feedback to gain competitive advantage. If this assumption holds true, improved market share could eventually translate into an improved financial picture for the firm. However, as this example illustrates, financial outcomes are somewhat removed from the actual implementation of 360° feedback, and thus, the connection between them becomes tenuous.

360° Feedback and Strategic Human Resources Management

A growing body of research addresses the issue of whether human resources management (HRM) policies and practices in general can affect aspects of organizational performance. Traditionally, when HRM has been associated with firm performance, practice has emphasized improving efficiency. This includes such issues as managing HR in an attempt to reduce turnover and its associated costs, designing compensation systems to minimize payroll costs, and staffing reduction methods.[2]

Less emphasis has been devoted to HRM as a means of value creation for organizations. In other words, do certain HRM policies and practices have the potential to increase quality, market share, revenue, and so forth for a company? Recent research gives credence to the notion that a company can indeed use HR as a source of competitive advantage but only by creating value in a manner that is difficult for competitors to imitate.[3]

A perplexing question comes to mind when considering the relationship between HRM and firm performance: Do certain HRM policies or practices work under any and all conditions to improve organizational performance, or does it depend on certain conditions? The idea that specific HRM methods can drive performance has a lot of intuitive appeal, perhaps because of its simplicity. For example, one might propose that 360° feedback programs improve organizational performance. However, as a complicating factor, companies typically do not implement such programs in the same manner. Uneven results across organizations might simply reflect unequal methods of implementation. Despite such problems, Jeff Pfeffer, a renowned organizational researcher, has argued that a *best practices* perspective will likely make the most sense. Researchers have the task of identifying those practices.[4]

Others have argued for a *contingency* approach to understanding the connection between HRM and organizational performance. This approach suggests that programs such as 360° feedback can impact performance, but the impact depends on certain conditions. For example, recent research has examined the impact of various HRM strategies on operational performance as conditioned by an organization's strategic posture.[5] These researchers suggested and found that the best HR system is contingent on the manufacturing strategy of a firm. Specifically, a capital-enhancing HR system affected performance primarily when the firm engaged in a quality-oriented manufacturing strategy. Capital-enhancing HR includes very selective staffing procedures, comprehensive training, behaviorally based appraisal mechanisms, skill- and group-based incentives, and so forth.

A *configural* perspective involves an even more complex approach to understanding the relationship between HR strategies and programs, such as 360° feedback, and organizational performance. Rather than attempting to focus on a key contingency factor, the *configural* perspective posits that one should consider a pattern of strategic, organizational, and HR-related factors. To be effective, an HR system, and specific practices and programs within that system, must achieve both vertical and horizontal fits. Vertical fit refers to the congruence of the HR system with other organizational and strategic characteristics. Horizontal fit pertains to the internal consistency of a firm's HR policies, practices, and programs. The ideal configuration is the one with the highest degree of overall fit.[6]

The remainder of this chapter will present a *configural* model of 360° feedback implementation and organizational performance. Although such an approach is more complex than either *best practices* or *contingency* perspectives, it provides the most realistic depiction of how 360° feedback could potentially impact performance. The simplicity of *best practices* and even *contingency* perspectives is appealing but, nevertheless, may not provide much help in understanding such a complex relationship.

A CONFIGURAL MODEL OF 360° FEEDBACK AND ORGANIZATIONAL PERFORMANCE

Before presenting the *configural* model, a straightforward acknowledgment is in order. The material presented here has an admittedly theoretical nature and, hence, can only provide a heuristic for thinking about the relationship between 360° feedback and organizational performance. Unfortunately, the authors know of no research that has systematically explored this relationship. They hope the present model will help guide future research efforts and that practitioners will gain insight into relevant managerial issues.

The model, shown in Exhibit 7-1, depicts four key elements that must come into alignment as a consistent pattern if 360° feedback efforts are to

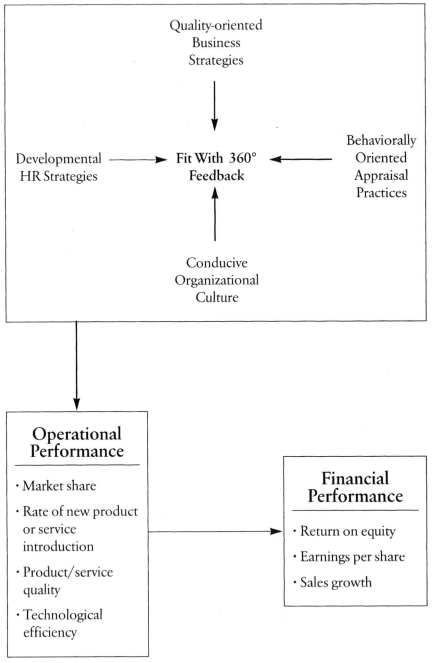

Exhibit 7-1. A Configural Framework of 360° Feedback and Organizational Performance

affect performance. Two of these elements represent aspects of vertical fit, and two represent aspects of horizontal fit. The sections below describe each type of fit with 360° feedback.

Vertical Fit

Conducive Culture. Three hundred sixty–degree feedback can affect performance, but only when aspects of the organization and its business strategies come into alignment with the implementation effort. One key aspect of the organization that must align well with a 360° initiative involves its culture. Chapter 6 discussed the connection between culture and 360° feedback at length. It considered how a 360° feedback initiative could improve organizational culture over time, but only under certain favorable conditions, such as current resolve among upper management. Chapter 6 referred to this as 360° feedback *pushing* organizational culture. Alternatively, a conducive organizational culture could simply *pull* a 360° feedback implementation effort along. In other words, 360° feedback could simply be seen as another program or tool fitting in neatly with an already conducive culture.

As evident in Exhibit 7-1, favorable performance effects will most likely occur in the latter condition, that is, when the already conducive organizational culture simply *pulls* the 360° feedback effort along. In such instances, fit already exists between culture and 360° feedback. In contrast, fit does not already exist when companies use 360° feedback to *push* culture change. In this case, the impact of 360° feedback may require a longer horizon.

Quality-oriented and Innovative Business Strategies. In addition to culture, appropriate fit with key business strategies may also prove relevant to the effect of 360° feedback on performance. Two such strategies appear especially important: (1) Quality orientation; and (2) Emphasis on innovation and flexibility.

Previous chapters have already considered a quality orientation, especially as it relates to organizational culture. However, one can also think of quality in terms of business strategy.[7] For example, many companies in recent years have chosen a quality orientation as a means of achieving competitive advantage in their markets.

One way to understand how a quality-oriented strategy can create fit with 360° feedback is to contrast it with a strategy devoted primarily to cost cutting. When a company primarily emphasizes cost cutting, it minimizes the value of human capital. Appraisal and feedback focus on error reduction, process standardization, and results only. Under such conditions, a developmental approach to appraisal and feedback, which could strengthen employee knowledge and skills, would likely have little utility.

In contrast, a quality-oriented strategy focuses on continuous improvement of processes and individuals. In this context, the ultimate determinant of competitiveness may lie in the intellectual capital of a company.[8] Output becomes highly sensitive to human knowledge and skills. As argued previously, 360° feedback can serve as an important lever for enhancing individuals' knowledge and skills. In short, the importance of such a lever becomes most apparent when a company pursues a quality-oriented strategy.

Readers especially familiar with writings associated with total quality management may perceive a paradox in the above logic. Specifically, one could view 360° feedback as just another form of performance appraisal, and many quality experts have scorned the use of performance appraisal.[9] However, such criticism is based on the traditional emphases placed on the results and administrative aspects of evaluation, while excluding or minimizing behavioral and developmental issues. Most recently, various writers have noted that appraisal plays an important developmental role in quality-oriented organizations.[10] For example, enhanced diagnosis and feedback are required if employees and managers are to achieve continuous improvement and better serve customer needs.

One can see much of the knowledge and skill enhancement so necessary as part of a quality-oriented strategy in the emphasis put on customer-supplier relationships (CSRs). Companies stress CSRs with regard to both internal customers, such as peers, coworkers, and subordinates, and external customers. When viewed as a relationship, it becomes apparent that to better serve customers, suppliers must have an awareness of those customers' problems and needs. Accordingly, 360° feedback can yield such information, thus providing knowledge and helping to build the skills so necessary for effective CSRs.

A related, yet somewhat different, form of business strategy involves innovation and flexibility. Companies that choose highly innovative strategies have been referred to as "prospectors."[11] Companies that rarely innovate are called "defenders." Along similar lines, flexible companies can scale production up and down, make quick changes in product or service mix, readily handle nonstandard orders, and so forth.[12]

Companies pursuing innovative, flexible strategies would be most likely to receive the performance benefits of 360° feedback. The unpredictable business environments faced by such companies require relatively rapid adjustments to meet the demands of customers. The communication engendered by 360° feedback would allow for a freer flow of information between peers, and peer groups, as they adapt to customers. As well, upward feedback from subordinates to managers would help ensure that the former has the power to serve the changing needs of customers and the latter leads and makes timely decisions. And obviously, information collected directly from external customers would assess whether those customers perceive that innovation and flexibility are truly being achieved.

To summarize, the vertical fit of organizational culture and business strategies is essential if companies are to realize the performance benefits of 360° feedback. However, there is more to the fit puzzle. Now attention turns to horizontal fit, or the internal consistency of a firm's HR policies and practices.

Horizontal Fit

When a company attempts to implement 360° degree feedback, it does not do so in an HR vacuum. In other words, 360° feedback exists within an array of guiding principles, policies, and practices that form the company's HR system. Practices, or programs, such as 360° feedback must properly align with other practices if they are to be consistent with the overall HR architecture.[13] Two key aspects of an HR architecture should be in place:

1. Developmental HR strategies; and
2. Behaviorally oriented appraisal practices.

Developmental HR Strategies. This book has stressed the importance of focusing 360° feedback efforts toward development rather than evaluation. A company can manifest an emphasis on development in a number of ways, aside from simply avoiding evaluative usages. In general, the 360° feedback process must go beyond simple surveying and providing feedback reports. A number of consulting companies have put most of their emphases on these aspects of the implementation process. However, to truly be developmental, ratees must be encouraged to seek additional feedback from raters, perhaps in a follow-up meeting. Perhaps facilita-

tors, such as human resource staff persons, could help guide such meetings. Developmental planning should also ensue whereby the ratee choos-
es specific areas to focus on in terms of improvement. A few organizations with particularly strong developmental strategies have assigned
mentors or coaches to guide ratees' developmental planning based on
feedback results.

A developmental strategy makes the most sense in an organization that
already places a great deal of emphasis on training and development.
Motorola, for example, devotes 1.5 percent of its budget to training and
requires every employee to receive forty hours of training every year. Such
organizations are characterized by significant amounts of employee and
managerial time devoted to continuous training activities. With regard to
360° feedback processes, the feedback data, follow-up sessions, and developmental planning may not be enough to ensure knowledge and skill
improvement. Typical areas in need of improvement include teamwork,
customer service, leadership, and interpersonal skills. A developmental
plan may need to include one or more training programs in such areas, and
accordingly, companies should make these programs available to ratees.

Behaviorally Oriented Appraisal Practices. Appraisal practices in organizations can have orientations toward either traits, results, or behaviors. A trait
orientation asks raters to make evaluations in terms of an individual's general qualities. Indeed, traditional appraisal forms have included such dimensions as dependability, optimism, friendliness, approachability, and the like.
Results-based appraisal places more of an emphasis on bottom-line performance, rather than asking raters to evaluate an individual's traits. For example, management-by-objectives appraisal methods have focused on planning performance around specific goals and then determining at the end of
a performance period whether the goals have been achieved.

Trait-oriented appraisal has been largely questioned because of the
vagueness of many traits that raters must evaluate and/or because of the
lack of psychological training on the part of raters that is necessary to evaluate others' traits. Results-based appraisal has received more support and,
indeed, has been shown to be at least somewhat related to organizational
performance.[14] There is no question that an emphasis on results can
achieve positive effects under many conditions. However, the most optimal configuration for 360° feedback will include an HR system largely oriented toward behavioral appraisal practices.

It is no accident that most of the 360° feedback instruments the
authors have viewed focus on behaviors. Ratings on behaviors provide

ratees a more specific basis upon which to improve, compared with ratings on traits. In addition, the behavioral orientation should extend beyond actual 360° feedback processes. Ideally, raters and ratees should already be accustomed to behaviorally oriented appraisal in their traditional appraisal systems prior to 360° feedback implementation. This would increase the likelihood of more accurate ratings and informative write-in comments on the part of raters.

In summary, the configural framework suggests that synergistic effects exist among HR practices that can only be achieved by maintaining consistency within the configuration. Moreover, consistency must be maintained between organizational culture, key business strategies, and the HR strategies and practices—including 360° feedback—if performance improvements are to be achieved. The HR strategies and practices discussed above form a pattern referred to as "human capital-enhancing."[15] Three hundred sixty—degree feedback fits in neatly with such a pattern because of its emphasis on developing and leveraging HR knowledge and skills through a focus on behaviors.

Operational vs. Financial Performance

A final note is warranted regarding the model of 360° feedback and organizational performance. Exhibit 7-1 shows how, with the proper configuration, 360° feedback may show relatively immediate effects on operational performance. For example, one should not have too much difficulty envisioning how the advent of 360° feedback could reveal problems pertaining to product or service quality, especially as viewed by customers. With effective developmental planning and coaching, one should expect to see improvements in quality.

On the other hand, financial performance may only be affected over the long term. That is, as shown in Exhibit 7-1, one would expect indirect effects between 360° feedback implementation and financial performance. The connection would only materialize over time as a result of initial improvements in operational performance.

CAVEATS AND CONCLUSIONS

One thing noticeably missing from this chapter has been specific evidence or examples of whether 360° feedback initiatives are indeed associated with organizational performance. As acknowledged earlier, the authors know of no such evidence, and herein lies a problem. An assumption prevalent among 360° feedback implementers maintains that positive performance effects will accrue. While this likely scenario may result, especially given the configuration outlined in this chapter, the jury remains out because systematic research remains to be conducted.

Part of the problem in providing such a test is that no universally accepted method of 360° feedback implementation exists. In essence, three scopes of involvement issues seem apparent. First, is it necessary to involve all possible 360° feedback sources? These sources can potentially include self, supervisor, subordinates, peers, and external customers. In reality, most implementation efforts have focused on the first three of these sources and, to a lesser extent, peers. Because of levels-of-analysis issues alluded to earlier, direct feedback from external customers to potential ratees has been limited.

Second, is it necessary to involve an entire organization, or could a company observe performance effects by only involving particular units or individual ratees? Logistically, administering 360° feedback to all potential ratees, especially in larger companies, may prove difficult. Perhaps it is only necessary to provide 360° feedback to those key ratees responsible for the operational performance indices shown in Exhibit 7-1.

Third, how often should a company administer 360° feedback? At a minimum, two administrations would allow ratees to obtain initial feedback and then make adjustments in their behavior. Moreover, at least six months should pass between administrations to allow these adjustments to occur. But additional administrations may prove necessary to truly enhance performance or maintain improvements in organizations that are using 360° feedback to *push* changes in the organizations' cultures.

In conclusion, 360° feedback programs hold much promise for organizations attempting to seek improvements in operational and financial performance. The authors hope this chapter has provided some insight into how such improvements can indeed come about. In the next and final chapter, attention turns toward the future in an attempt to understand where this innovation in organizational feedback and communication may head.

REFERENCES

1. For a more complete discussion of measures of organizational performance, see N. Venkatraman and V. Ramanujam, "Measurement of Business Performance in Strategy Research: A Comparison of Approaches," *Academy of Management Review*, 11 (1986), pp. 801–814.

2. For a consideration of HRM as a means of cost reduction versus value creation, see B. Becker and B. Gerhart, "The Impact of Human Resource Management on Organizational Performance: Progress and Prospects," *Academy of Management Journal*, 39 (1996), pp. 779–801.

3. This idea of HR as a source of competitive advantage is contained within the resource-based view of the firm. For more information, see J. Barney, "Firm Resources and Sustained Competitive Advantage," *Journal of Management*, 17 (1991), pp. 99-120.

4. See J. Pfeffer, *Competitive Advantage Through People* (Boston: Harvard Business School Press, 1994).

5. See M. A. Youndt, et al., "Human Resource Management, Manufacturing Strategy, and Firm Performance," *Academy of Management Journal*, 39 (1996), pp. 836–866.

6. For a more detailed consideration of contingency versus configural perspectives, see J. E. Delery and D. H. Doty, "Modes of Theorizing in Strategic Human Resource Management: Tests of Universalistic, Contingency, and Configural Performance Predictions," *Academy of Management Journal*, 39 (1996), pp. 802–835.

7. For an in-depth discussion of quality in terms of both culture and strategy, see J. W. Dean, Jr., and J. Evans, *Total Quality: Management, Organization, and Strategy* (St. Paul: West, 1994).

8. Youndt, et al., op cit.

9. As an example, see W. E. Deming, *Out of the Crisis* (Cambridge, Mass.: MIT Center for Advanced Engineering Study, 1986).

10. The importance of appraisal and 360° feedback in quality initiatives has been considered recently by:
   D. A. Waldman, "Designing Performance Management Systems for Total Quality Implementation," *Journal of Organizational Change Management*, 7(2) (1994), pp. 31–44.
   J. Ghorpade and M. M. Chen, "Creating Quality-driven Performance Appraisal Systems," *Academy of Management Executive*, 91 (1995), pp. 32–41.

11. This term comes from a popular theory of business strategy put forth by R. E. Miles and C. C. Snow, *Organizational Strategy, Structure, and Process* (New York: McGraw-Hill, 1978).

12. Youndt, et al., op cit.

13. The authors borrowed this term from Becker and Gerhart, op cit.

14. Delery and Doty, op cit.

15. Youndt, et al., op cit.

CHAPTER 8

What Is the Future of 360° Feedback?

Probably the most difficult task with regard to any management or HR innovation involves the attempt to look into the future to determine where it might head. Three hundred sixty-degree feedback is no exception. While no one has a crystal ball, a number of recent trends and indicators provide clues as to the direction of 360° feedback.

DYING FAD OR EMERGING SCIENCE?

The most basic issue is whether 360° feedback has reached its peak and has now started down the painful road of another dying, or at least fading, management fad. Alternatively, and more optimistically, does 360° feedback represent an emerging science about which HR professionals will continue to gain understanding and expertise? Where will 360° feedback be in ten years?

Current organizational trends regarding 360° feedback can help provide clues about its future. The authors' best estimates of *current* organizational participation rates follow:

1. Organizations that tried it and subsequently dropped it (10 percent);

2. Organizations that tried it and institutionalized it (10 percent);

3. Organizations currently considering implementing it (30 percent);

4. Organizations that have no interest in it (30 percent); and

5. Organizations that do not know it exists (20 percent).

These percentages represent a best guess and are not based on survey results. They also probably have more accuracy with regard to larger organizations. Ten years from now, the same statistics might look like this:

1. Organizations that will have tried it and subsequently dropped it (25 percent);

2. Organizations that will have tried it and institutionalized it (35 percent);

3. Organizations that will be considering implementing it (20 percent);

4. Organizations that will have no interest in it (15 percent); and

5. Organizations that will not know it exists (5 percent).

In other words, more organizations will have tried it. Some will continue to see little merit or will not believe it is worth the expense. More will have tried it and abandoned it for a variety of reasons. More than a third will have institutionalized it.

One thing apparent from these predictions is that the authors simultaneously predict increases in the dropping of 360° feedback programs, as well as the institutionalization of such efforts. How could such a paradox manifest itself? What current trends could lead to a decline, and conversely, do trends exist that could lead to further institutionalization of 360° feedback?

Threats to the Emerging Science

Do threats to the continuing proliferation of 360° feedback initiatives exist that could cause an increase in the number of firms abandoning such efforts? Unfortunately, indeed some real threats reside not in the inherent nature of 360° feedback, but rather in the lack of systematic knowledge regarding how to best implement it and under what circumstances.

One issue stressed repeatedly throughout this book is that firms should move slowly and cautiously in terms of using 360° feedback for evaluative purposes. Some organizations will likely abandon their 360° feedback initiatives in the future because lawsuits alleging the unfairness of the process have legally "burned" them. Aspects of the process that ratees could potentially challenge in court include the anonymous nature of raters. Moreover, if raters, for example subordinates, receive retribution for low scores provided to ratees, for example supervisors, the raters themselves could grieve and/or sue.

Evaluative aspects of performance appraisal, in general, will likely become less important to organizations in the future. According to one recent *Wall Street Journal* article, companies are beginning to question why they currently use performance appraisal in such an evaluative manner.[1] That article posed the question, "If 85 percent of your customers were dissatisfied with your product, would you get rid of it?" As it turns out, 85 percent of managers feel dissatisfied with traditional, evaluative performance appraisal practices. So why is the traditional performance appraisal still so popular? It is not accomplishing much of what it intends to, is often manipulated, and does not seem to protect companies from lawsuits.

A number of writers recently suggested that firms at least simplify performance appraisal such that only the few individuals *clearly* performing below standards are differentiated for evaluative purposes. Likewise, a company might also differentiate positively those few performing clearly above standards.[2] At the least, firms seeking to make 360° feedback evaluative might consider such a conservative approach.

Employers should recognize that they will not likely accomplish the developmental and evaluative purposes of 360° feedback simultaneously. Rather, they will have to make a choice. A recent study reported that 40 percent of the people providing 360° ratings said they would have altered those ratings if the company planned to use them for evaluation.[3] Probably, these alterations would move in the direction of less honesty, perhaps some more critical and others less critical. Regardless, when used for evaluation, raters will likely compromise the honesty needed for optimal development purposes .

Other aspects of 360° feedback implementation processes would benefit from additional research. These include:

1. How to give and receive good feedback;

2. The importance of follow-up feedback and clarification from those providing ratings;

3. How often to administer 360° feedback in organizations to maintain employee interest and continue the development process;

4. When in one's career does 360° feedback have the most impact in terms of improving behavior; and

5. How raters interpret ratings from various sources, that is, which ratings do they give the most weight in their formulations of development plans.

Opportunities for an Emerging Science

One reason for the prediction of more experimentation with, and institutionalization of, 360° feedback is that one can view it as a continuing, historic trend. As elaborated upon in Chapter 1, the process of surveying in organizations has been going on for a long time, and there is no reason to expect this trend to cease. Accordingly, there is reason to believe that since 360° feedback fits neatly within this continuing tradition, it should flourish for years to come.

Employee demand for 360° feedback will also likely increase. People tend to fear change and the unknown. Several years ago 360° feedback could fall into such a category. However, as it becomes more institutionalized, raters and ratees will become accustomed to providing and receiving feedback, respectively. As those who get the feedback improve their behaviors and performance, others will desire the process in order to keep up. Similarly, interest in spreading the process to all levels in the organization including lowest-level employees, or peer feedback, will increase. Finally, the authors have heard frequent calls from organizational members asking for the ability to provide skip-level upward feedback to managers one or more levels above one's own supervisor.

Partnerships between academics and practitioners represent a key opportunity in the emerging science of 360° feedback. To date, such partnerships have been relatively rare. Instead, partnerships have typically occurred in the form of contracted services between consulting firms and client firms. This book does not intend criticality of consulting firms and their products or services. At the same time, consulting firms primarily make a business of selling those products or services in line with the stated demands of their clients. Only secondarily do they make a business of questioning those demands or conducting research to better understand the organizational dynamics associated with processes such as 360° feedback. Besides, they are rewarded—paid—for delivering products or services. They typically do not receive rewards for conducting rigorous formal evaluations that may show that their products or services do not work so well.[4]

As such, one should not be surprised to observe that most consulting efforts, and thus many implementation efforts to date, focus almost entirely on the actual surveying and compilation of feedback reports. Furthermore, companies typically use off-the-shelf surveys and feed-back report designs. By now, the reader should have realized that 360° feedback has far greater organizational ramifications. Organizations must take a variety of other issues into account if they expect 360° feedback to have positive organizational outcomes. These issues include evaluative versus developmental usages, extent of existing cynicism toward change efforts, whether the existing culture is conducive, attempts at follow-up after receiving initial feedback information, and developmental planning efforts.

As stated above, a variety of important issues and questions remain unresolved with regard to the effective implementation of 360° feedback processes. Academics tend to have the background and motivation to address these issues in a systematic manner. Thus, partnerships between academics and practitioners attempting to implement 360° feedback seem warranted. By engaging in such partnerships, academics could help further the emerging science, while practitioners would gain valuable insights into how or whether the 360° feedback processes work.

As described briefly in Chapters 1 and 6, the authors recently entered into a partnership with a state policing organization. The purpose of the partnership is to systematically study various aspects of an upward feed-back process and its effects on aspects of the organization. For example, the authors will analyze whether behavior change can occur by simply sur-veying raters and ratees, thus allowing them to see specific behaviors con-sidered important by the organization. Or, conversely, is such surveying in and of itself insufficient? That is, must ratees also receive feedback forms and/or engage in additional feedback-seeking behavior to make significant behavioral changes?

Two unique aspects emerge from this project. First, the organization has allowed the authors to include a control group at Time 1. The project involves Time 1 and Time 2 administrations, approximately eight months apart. While some research has included multiple administrations, the authors know of no 360° feedback research that used a control group in a field setting. Organizations often hesitate to use a control group because they feel if an initiative is worth applying, it is worth applying evenly across the organization. Moreover, they fear members will perceive unequal treat-ment and, hence, inequities. This particular policing organization has cooperated quite well and is eager to understand the dynamics of feedback processes. Second, the authors are assessing a number of organizationally based contingency factors and outcome measures, including group and organizational commitment, cynicism toward organizational change, and unit-level performance.

To illustrate the partnership nature of the project, over the long term the authors plan to include peer ratings of police officers and ratings from external customers, or community members. In short, they expect the project to grow and provide benefits not only to the client organization but also the emerging science of 360° feedback.

ADDITIONAL TRENDS

One can envision a number of additional trends in the realm of 360° feedback as one looks toward the future. For example, easier data entry and feedback procedures will continue to evolve over time so involvement of individuals outside the feedback process, that is, people other than raters and ratees, will not be needed. In its first few administrations of 360° feedback, an organization will still need outsiders to help individuals work through the initial problems and emotions involved, but as it becomes routine within that organization, outside involvement will no longer prove necessary.

With the increase in team-based structures in organizations, feedback instruments designed specifically for team members to receive feedback from one another about their team behaviors and performance will become more popular. The authors' own organization, Atwater Management Consulting, has developed an instrument called the TEAM-Q, which provides team feedback to each team member about his or her contributions to the team and collaboration skills as a team member. This instrument also assesses team members' perceptions of the extent to which systems exist within an organization to support the team's efforts. These types of instruments will increase in popularity. Appendix B provides a sample of this TEAM-Q instrument.

Involvement of public sector organizations in the 360° process will increase. It seems that most 360° feedback interventions to date have been in the private sector, but as the process becomes more visible and imperfections are worked out, public sector interest will grow. Currently, in addition to the police organization, the authors are working with a city government agency implementing 360° feedback for supervisors.

Three hundred sixty-degree feedback will provide particular value to public sector and service organizations. Because many public sector and service organizations lack a clear or tangible product, they have more difficulty assessing performance. Therefore, they have more difficulty giving accurate and useful performance feedback. The leadership, interpersonal, and customer service factors generally assessed with 360° instruments will provide valuable feedback to those whose performance yields services that are difficult to measure. Moreover, quality performance in such jobs is more difficult to measure, compared with work involving tangible products. Three hundred sixty–degree feedback can provide customer-based alternative indices of quality.

In sum, 360° feedback will not disappear like an unpopular flavor of ice cream. Nor will it flourish and be implemented everywhere. Rather, those organizations that have discovered the fit between their cultures, practices, and 360° feedback will institutionalize it, and those embracing it to keep up with the Joneses may drop it. Nevertheless, after ten more years of collaboration between industry and academia, the authors hope they can write a book titled *The Successes and Failures of 360° Feedback: How 360° Feedback Impacts the Bottom Line.*

REFERENCES

1. Timothy D. Schellhardt, "It's Time to Evaluate Your Work, and All Involved Are Groaning," *The Wall Street Journal,* 228(100) (November 19, 1996), pp. A1, A10.

2. The issue of making performance appraisal less evaluative through the simplification of evaluative differentiation has been argued at length by D. A. Waldman, "Designing Performance Management Systems for Total Quality Implementation," *Journal of Organizational Change Management,* 7(2) (1994), pp. 31–44.

3. M. London and J. Smither, "Can Multisource Feedback Change Self-evaluations, Skill Development, and Performance? Theory-based Applications and Directions for Research," *Personnel Psychology,* 48 (1995), pp. 803–839.

4. Steve Kerr shows how the use of consultants can illustrate the old problem of "rewarding A, while hoping for B." See S. Kerr, "On the Folly of Rewarding A, While Hoping for B," *Academy of Management Executive,* 9(1) (1995), pp. 7–14.

APPENDIX A

Typical 360° Feedback Survey Items and Report

Sample of Typical 360° Survey Items

Please indicate how often this manager engages in each of the following activities or behaviors. ● **Personal Effectiveness**	Not applicable	Not at all		Once in a while		Sometimes		Fairly often			Almost always
1. Accepts feedback without becoming defensive (e.g., making excuses, denial, getting angry)	NA	1	2	3	4	5	6	7	8		9
2. Is appropriately concerned about how his/her behavior affects others	NA	1	2	3	4	5	6	7	8		9
3. Is frank and honest in his/her dealings with others	NA	1	2	3	4	5	6	7	8		9
4. Makes tough decisions in a timely manner	NA	1	2	3	4	5	6	7	8		9
5. Treats people consistently; doesn't show favoritism	NA	1	2	3	4	5	6	7	8		9
6. Is available when needed	NA	1	2	3	4	5	6	7	8		9
7. Helps plan and organize the workflow of the work group........	NA	1	2	3	4	5	6	7	8		9

This is a sample of a page from a survey that would be completed by a subordinate of the target manager. Each assessment source (self, subordinates, peers, supervisors, etc.) would receive a similar form tailored to fit that group.

Items can easily be modified or added.

Other dimensions (e.g., leadership, teamwork, interpersonal skills, etc.) would also be assessed.

Concise, constructive, open-ended questions could also be included. For example:

"List the three most effective strengths of the person you rated in this survey."

"List the three areas in which the person you rated could use more development."

360° Feedback Summary for A. SAMPLE

PERSONAL EFFECTIVENESS

	AVERAGES				COMPARISONS*			COUNT OF ALL RESPONSES (EXCEPT SELF)									
	SELF 1	YOUR MGRS 3	PEERS 4	SUBS 5	YOUR MGRS Minus ALL MGRS	YOUR PEERS Minus ALL PEERS	YOUR SUBS Minus ALL SUBS	NA	LOW 1	2	3	4	5	6	7	8	HIGH 9
1. Accepts feedback without becoming defensive (e.g., making excuses, denial, getting angry).	7	8.3	8.0	7.2	0.6	0.5	0.1	0	0	0	0	0	0	0	3	3	5
2. Is appropriately concerned about how his/her behavior affects others.	7	8.3	8.7	8.5	0.7	1.2	1.6	2	0	0	0	0	0	2	3	3	5
3. Is frank and honest in his/her dealings with others.	8	8.0	8.0	6.0	0.2	0.0	-1.4	0	0	0	1	0	0	1	2	3	5
4. Makes tough decisions in a timely manner.	7	6.0	5.8	5.8	-1.2	-1.9	-1.6	0	1	0	0	3	2	6	0	0	0
5. Treats people consistently; doesn't show favoritism.	6	8.7	8.8	8.0	1.0	1.3	0.9	0	0	0	0	0	0	1	1	7	4
6. Is available when needed.	8	8.0	7.8	7.4	0.0	0.2	0.0	0	0	0	0	0	1	0	4	4	3
7. Helps plan and organize the workflow of the work group effectively.	7	6.7	5.8	6.4	-0.8	-2.2	-1.0	0	0	0	0	1	2	3	5	1	0

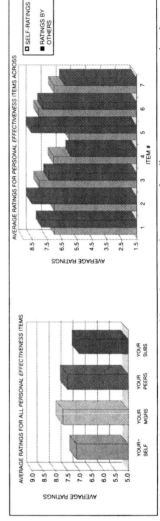

AVERAGE RATINGS FOR ALL PERSONAL EFFECTIVENESS ITEMS

AVERAGE RATINGS FOR PERSONAL EFFECTIVENESS ITEMS ACROSS

SELF-RATINGS
RATINGS BY OTHERS

* The scores in these columns are created by subtracting the average for all managers, peers, or subordinates from the feedback recipient's score received from his/her managers/peers/subordinates.

Typical TEAM-Q Survey Items and Feedback Report

SAMPLE OF TYPICAL TEAM-Q SURVEY ITEMS

As illustrated by the sample survey items below, all team members first assess themselves and other team members on collaboration skills and contributions to the team. Then they provide ratings of organizational systems and managerial practices that can impact team effectiveness.

In the first section, the employee evaluates himself/herself and team members on collaboration and contribution.

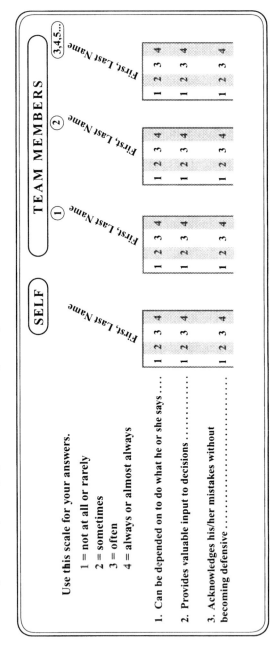

Use this scale for your answers.

1 = not at all or rarely
2 = sometimes
3 = often
4 = always or almost always

1. Can be depended on to do what he or she says . . . .

2. Provides valuable input to decisions . . . .

3. Acknowledges his/her mistakes without becoming defensive . . . .

Space for written comments about team members is provided.

If you have specific comments about any team member, please provide them, along with the team member's name, in the space provided.

The next set of questions addresses organizational issues such as management practices and organizational systems.

22. Team members have an adequate say in selecting team members.	1	2 3	4
23. Systems are in place to allow the team adequate access to other groups on which it depends . .	1	2 3	4
24. The team receives adequate recognition for its accomplishments.	1	2 3	4

Space for written comments about the organization is also provided.

In the space provided please include additional, more detailed comments about managerial or support systems that impact team performance.

SAMPLE TEAM-Q FEEDBACK REPORT

Each team member receives a confidential report showing his/her scores and normative information.

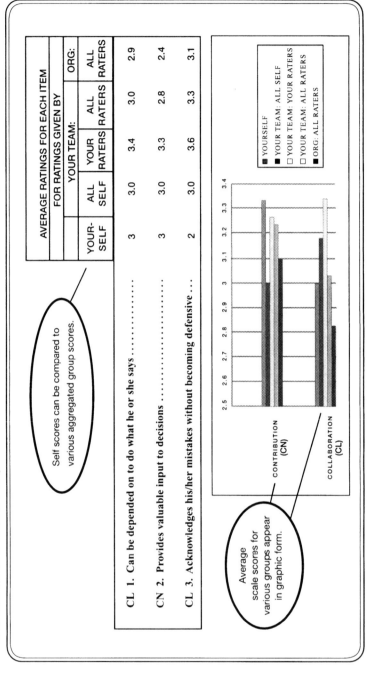

Self scores can be compared to various aggregated group scores.

	AVERAGE RATINGS FOR EACH ITEM				
		FOR RATINGS GIVEN BY			ORG:
		YOUR TEAM:			
	YOUR-SELF	ALL SELF	YOUR RATERS	ALL RATERS	ALL RATERS
CL 1. Can be depended on to do what he or she says	3	3.0	3.4	3.0	2.9
CN 2. Provides valuable input to decisions	3	3.0	3.3	2.8	2.4
CL 3. Acknowledges his/her mistakes without becoming defensive	2	3.0	3.6	3.3	3.1

Average scale scores for various groups appear in graphic form.

■ YOURSELF
■ YOUR TEAM: ALL SELF
□ YOUR TEAM: YOUR RATERS
□ YOUR TEAM: ALL RATERS
■ ORG: ALL RATERS

CONTRIBUTION (CN)

COLLABORATION (CL)

This next section addresses ratings of management practices and organizational systems for each team compared to all other teams in the organization.

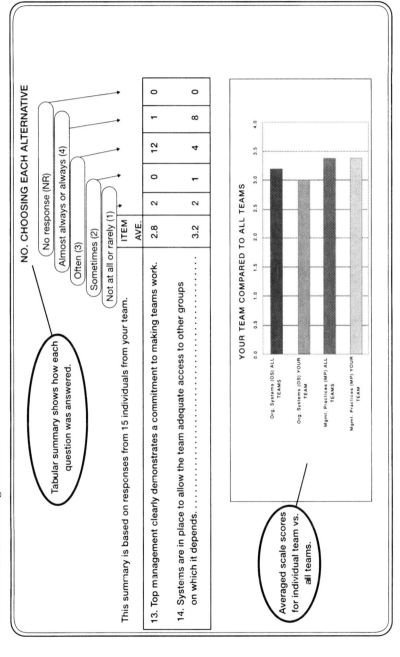

NO. CHOOSING EACH ALTERNATIVE

Tabular summary shows how each question was answered.

This summary is based on responses from 15 individuals from your team.

	ITEM AVE.	Not at all or rarely (1)	Sometimes (2)	Often (3)	Almost always or always (4)	No response (NR)
13. Top management clearly demonstrates a commitment to making teams work.	2.8	2	0	12	1	0
14. Systems are in place to allow the team adequate access to other groups on which it depends.	3.2	2	1	4	8	0

YOUR TEAM COMPARED TO ALL TEAMS

Averaged scale scores for individual team vs. all teams.

Index

Printed in the United Kingdom
by Lightning Source UK Ltd.
128561UK00001B/7/A